T0319979

GOODS

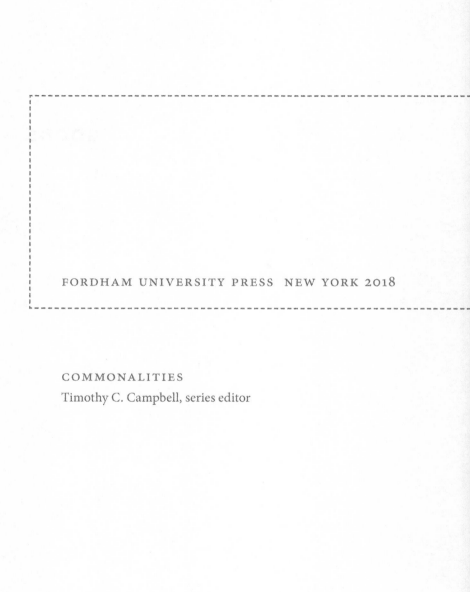

FORDHAM UNIVERSITY PRESS   NEW YORK 2018

COMMONALITIES
Timothy C. Campbell, series editor

GOODS

*Advertising, Urban Space, and
the Moral Law of the Image*

EMANUELE COCCIA

Translated by Marissa Gemma

Copyright © 2018 Fordham University Press

All rights reserved. No part of this publication may be reproduced, stored in a retrieval system, or transmitted in any form or by any means—electronic, mechanical, photocopy, recording, or any other—except for brief quotations in printed reviews, without the prior permission of the publisher.

Goods was originally published in French as *La Bien dans les choses* by Editions Payot & Rivages in 2013 and in Italian as *Il Bene nelle cose* by Il Mulino, in 2014. © 2013 Emanuele Coccia; © 2013 Editions Payot & Rivages.

The translation of this work has been funded by SEPS
SEGRETARIATO EUROPEO PER LE PUBBLICAZIONI SCIENTIFICHE

Via Val d'Aposa 7 - 40123 Bologna - Italy
seps@seps.it - www.seps.it

Fordham University Press has no responsibility for the persistence or accuracy of URLs for external or third-party Internet websites referred to in this publication and does not guarantee that any content on such websites is, or will remain, accurate or appropriate.

Fordham University Press also publishes its books in a variety of electronic formats. Some content that appears in print may not be available in electronic books.

Visit us online at www.fordhampress.com.

Library of Congress Control Number: 2018934476

Printed in the United States of America

20 19 18   5 4 3 2 1

First edition

CONTENTS

PREFACE TO THE ENGLISH-LANGUAGE EDITION

We used to think that we only had societies and governments because we had language. We used to think that we were only political beings because we could speak. In the language of ancient Greece, a person is a *zoon politikon* only because she is a *zoon logon echon*. This opinion has been widespread in modern political philosophy and was prevalent among the ancient Greeks. In one of the first political science treatises produced by Western culture, Aristotle remarks that if the *polis* (the state or city) "belongs among the things that exist by nature," and if "man is by nature a political animal"—much more political "than any kind of bee or any herd animal"—it's because "man alone among the animals has language." It's through language that we can have "a perception of good and bad and just and unjust and other things [of this sort]." Only if we share this kind of judgment is it possible to conceive of a city—or, for that matter, of a household.

Roman civilization gave a special name to language's power to establish a *political* community: *ius*, law. The term referred not to language in general, but to a series of formulas, a collection of stereotypical expressions that were treated as the formal source of social life. What we have since then called "the law" is nothing more than socially efficacious language, which is thought to be capable of shaping human life through its very existence and pronouncement. Living under the rule of law means living in a society that has cordoned off a number of socially efficacious words and discourses: it has isolated them physically, separating them from other words by locating them within the bounds of the law. The rule of law is the public and collective worship of these words, a worship that recognizes in them a form of secular sacredness.

Modern political philosophy has specified that it is not language or the law in general, but a special kind of linguistic act, a special kind of legal institution, which make a state possible: what we call *contracts* (or constitutions). A state can arise thanks to a particular type of promise that concerns not just a limited group but the totality of individuals; a state puts together each individual's power.

Though these observations may seem obvious, we have never had a clear idea of why or how language would be able to *make* us by nature more political than bees or herd animals. It is no easy matter to explicate Aristotle's position clearly. And the power of the law is also far from obvious. The sets of words that we collect into law books have no special formal features: they do not differ from other words in terms of language and grammar, nor are they distinct in meaning or style. What transforms them into the object of collective worship is an extensive set of myths that justifies their existence and is often part of the legislative corpus. The most famous examples of this phenomenon come from the Jewish and Christian legal traditions. Most of the stories in the two major law books of antiquity, the Jewish *Tanakh* and the Christian Bible, are myths that try to establish that law can only exist in the guise of a Word and that the true and holy community is the one based on the worship of the word, which is represented in one case as a sacred book and in the other as embodied in a Messiah. Norms not only have to be made out of words, but they also represent the Word par excellence, the one that embodies the (divine) rationality responsible for the creation of the universe. The myth of creation is a juridical one: it proves that there is a perfect continuity between the juridical techne and the ontogenic one, and a perfect coincidence of subjects in the legislator and the producer of reality—and reality is the object of the law.

It is not enough to say that the idea that our political life is founded on language is a myth. Levi Strauss has taught us that every myth should be read as the contrastive transformation of another one: no myth has meaning in itself, beyond its opposition to another myth. In Jewish-Christian legal mythology, the idea that the law takes shape in language arises in direct opposition to the idea of rules embodied in *images* or objects. The Word is the universal antidote to the normative power of images—to what I propose to call iconic normativity, condemned by the theological tradition as idolatry.

The influence of the Jewish and Christian legal tradition on the modern political experience is much broader than historians usually like to admit.

Our societies still harbor an unreflective suspicion of images and their founding role in political life. When Guy Debord introduces the "social relation among people mediated by images"—that is, the power of images to produce society, establishing the foundation of our political life as a spectacle, or as "the concrete inversion of life, the autonomous movement of the non-living"—he is simply giving voice to this ancestral myth.

What if this other, now obscure tradition was right? What if images were not a symptom of our society's alienation, as the French moralist tradition from Rousseau to Virilio has always thought, but were rather the conditions of possibility for our political life? I propose the term *micro-ontology* to describe the way politics would look if we recognized that we can build what we call a state, a city, or an institution—and along with them, we can access the political sphere—not through language but through images, in all their forms—that is, through our sensible life. To use the language of our legal and political culture, I would put it like this: what would life be like if we had social pictures instead of social contracts? Or, to put it more provocatively: what would our political life look like if the Messiah, the divine king who was supposed to embody the law, had left us not a biography but a documentary film or a collection of icons? Due to constraints of space, my remarks here will be extremely brief and rudimentarily elliptic. I will proceed in three steps. First, I will describe the consequences of this idea (that is, of the idea that we are *zoa politika* only because we can produce sensory experiences—not only pictures, but sounds, smells, all kind of sensible life). Next, I will describe what an iconic normativity would look like. What would a form of law that consists only of images look like? Finally, I will consider what the political life of the individual looks like when norms and political life are made from images. My general hypothesis is that an iconic politics is already at work in contemporary Western societies.

HOW TO DO THINGS WITH IMAGES

In order to understand what is or would be the nature of politics if it were based on images and not on language, we have to avoid one mistake: this is not just a matter of replacing the faculty of language with the human faculty of imagination. It is about recognizing that if there is something that we can call politics, it's because of the very existence of images, whether human or not (as Chiara Bottici has shown in a very important book).[1] Images are not a human faculty, in the double sense that they are not necessarily an expression of a human ability (the image of my body in a mirror doesn't depend on one of my faculties), nor are they exclusively human. If images can establish political life and enable its existence, it's because they are a reality, ontologically separated from man. The political is a property of images prior to being a human dimension: human beings can participate in political life only thanks to images—thanks to their relationship to images. Politics is the being of images. To think of images as the foundation of our political life means therefore first of all to investigate the images' specific mode of being. Following an ancient philosophical tradition, images should not be considered as mere cognitive devices or as things in themselves. They are, rather, a special kind of being, a sphere of the real that is separate from the other spheres; something that exists in itself and possesses a particular way of being, whose form urgently needs to be described. For this reason, politics as the science of images is a special kind of minor ontology—a micro-ontology, capable of positing another kind of being, the being of images beyond the being of things, of mind, and of consciousness.

Politics is a micro-ontology because, as philosophy has always held, images have a minor being, inferior to the thing of which they are the image. The iconic being is an extremely weak one (*esse debile*) in comparison to the being of the thing itself or that of subjects or of the mind. Images are the weakest and most fragile form of being that exists in the universe. If politics is the being of images, politics has a minor being: that's why the political sphere is always so fragile and vulnerable—it consists of images.

The second feature of the nature of images—which can help us to understand or rethink politics—is their medial character. The being of images exists somewhere between the being of things and the being of souls, between bodies and spirit. Forms that exist outside of the soul have a purely corporeal being, while those that exist within the soul have a purely spiritual being. Images are necessary for this very reason, because they constitute the mediation that permits nature to pass from the spiritual to the corporeal domain, and vice versa. For this reason, the first *aporetic evidence* of politics considered as a question of images (and not of words) is that it is not a science of subjects nor a science of objects; it is equally distinct and distant from psychology and economy, from neuroscience and technology. We have a political life because we have access to this sphere, which is neither purely subjective nor purely objective. Conversely, politics is the place where everything must assume this intermediary status: it is not the activity of humanizing the world (what geologists nowadays call anthropocenic activity), nor of objectifying the human (the science or activity of producing and managing things), but rather the process of reproducing the human and the natural in a separate sphere.

WHEN NORMS ARE IMAGES: ADVERTISING

If politics consists of images—if images can establish the political sphere—this is due to a special power that images have; what we usually call law should then be seen as a peculiar emanation of this power.

The power of the image has been studied at length (D. Freedberg, W. J. T. Mitchell, P. Zanker[2]) and described in terms of the image's ability to consolidate habits and judgments of taste. Considering this power from a juridical point of view allows us to overcome the opposition between its roots in nature (images do exercise their power by nature, that is, because of their active essence or because of the brain's peculiar capacity to respond to them) and its roots in culture (images acquire power only in relation to a specific historical and cultural context). Law is both a universal anthropological feature (every society has a normative system) based on natural social phenomena (commandments, rules, obedience) and a cultural feature, subject to change and taking on different structures in different contexts.

When embodied in images, normativity has to be viewed in the largest sense, as a set of norms whose object is human life in its totality, and not just a portion of it, such as single actions or the interaction between subjects (litigations), as was the case in Roman law. Also, when embodied in images, a norm cannot be immediately identified as a commandment. After all, legal systems in Western countries have always comprehended the spheres of persuasion and advising as integral parts of the system and have given those spheres a weight equal to the rules themselves. The opposition between the obligatory (*praeceptum*) and the advisory (*consilium*) is inherent in the law and does not coincide with the opposition between the juridical and the nonjuridical. Advice, recommendations, and warnings have always been just as "legal" as rules, orders, and obligations. We have considered persuasion to be a task for the law just as much as carrying out the law is.

Engaging with the notion of iconic normativity (of a norm based on and embodied purely in images) is far from an idle imaginative exercise: in modern globalized societies, images—much more than words—are responsible for shaping social customs and practices.[3] The dominance of iconic communication in social networks such as Instagram or Snapchat is a symptom of this very phenomenon. Conversely, whereas in the past images may have had a mainly aesthetic, decorative, or (more rarely) cognitive purpose,[4] today they operate more and more as the organs of a new form of collective normativity and individual psychagogy. The deepest and most effective social rules are nowadays formulated via images—that is, iconically.[5] This phenomenon is not entirely new: of course, there have been cultures and traditions that persistently relied upon images to formulate and transmit not simply knowledge, but "all the forms of normative knowledge: morality, religion, politics";[6] and in Western culture, there have been iconic expressions of moral and juridical sciences (like emblems, to take one example).[7]

But in contemporary Western societies there is a specific laboratory in which we produce and develop iconic normativity: advertising. Advertising first understood that images could embody rules, that they could represent a new kind of legal body; advertising first transformed the infinite power of images into a normative power. Advertising helped to translate the large set of social rules and habits that shaped Western societies into iconic form. Conversely, what we have called "advertising" since World War II ought to be seen not as a secondary, ambiguous, and unaccountable by-product of late capitalism, but rather as the sphere in which images went beyond their merely aesthetic and cognitive functions and acquired a normative role. Advertising has always considered itself to be the most influential and powerful agent of social change and social structuring. "Advertising modifies the course of a people's daily thoughts," one can read in one of the first modern treatises on advertising; it "gives them new words, new phrases, new ideas, new fashions, new prejudices and new customs. . . . It may be doubted if any other one force, the school, the church and the press excepted, has so great an influence as advertising."[8]

For contemporary Western societies, advertising is a powerful open-air laboratory that produces socially relevant images, and advertising images are the most copious and widespread set of images such a society has. Thus, they also are the most commonly seen and consumed images, to a much greater extent than any other artistic or cultural images. They have to convey the social desires, shared dreams, common needs, and ambitions of a large part of civil society. In this sense, advertising produces an important portion of the iconic culture of Western society. Nevertheless, it is not easy to define such images. They cannot be recognized and separated from other types of images or iconic structures on the basis of their proper content (an exclusive object), nor because they have a special form (a specialized language) or a unique message (selling or shopping suggestions). The growth of advertising in the West has dramatically widened the number and the variety of represented objects: everything—every object in common use, including rare or embarrassing ones (from cars to sanitary pads, from socks to laxatives)—is now represented, now exists in image form. Everything becomes visible through advertising. Furthermore, *pace* semiotics, any image can become an ad: this is strikingly demonstrated by Oliviero Toscani, who, borrowing from Warhol, transformed photojournalism into advertising images. Finally, the ironic nature of advertising communication allows it to express any kind of message, including anticapitalist ones (as exemplified by the recent collaboration of Abercrombie & Fitch with Marxist Slovenian philosopher Slavoj Žižek). That is to say, an image becomes an advertising image precisely because of its normative task. In analyzing the normative character of advertising images, two sets of questions arise. On the one hand, the idea that norms are exclusively linguistic in nature can be questioned: what would a legal system that produces norms only via iconic items look like? The hypothesis I offer is that an iconic norm cannot be characterized by the preceptive quality of verbal norms. The efficacy of social images in consolidating habits and taste judgments could be considered from a normative and juridical point of view. On the other hand, investigating advertising images would allow us to understand what an image is when its task is no longer the communication of information (i.e., a cognitive task) nor the production of aesthetic feelings of pleasure or displeasure, but the realization of a norm.

"Advertising . . . has a history as old as that of the human race. Just as soon as there were enough people in the world, some sort of formal announcement had to be made."[9] Far from being a modern pathological excrescence of public space or a symptom of the social pathologies of late capitalism, advertising is the contemporary form assumed by an ever-present discourse. The thesis of the book is that the spaces that today host a discourse incessantly talking of and displaying all the things that we call commodities were used in ancient times to honor and sanctify the gods, the city, and the dead—that is, the spaces that were used for epigraphic and monumental iconography. And just like ancient epigraphic literature, advertising has a moral purpose: it has to shape public morality and the civic self-consciousness, to form the ethos of the polis, to name and glorify its values. What has changed is the subject of this monumental literature. If epigraphic iconography was a reflexive iconic space where a society spoke of itself and its values and represented itself in an idealized or divinized form, in advertising the representation of the supreme moral values of a city coincides with representations of commodities. Things are represented as the cause of individual and common wealth and happiness: they are the personification of goodness and moral values. Paradoxically speaking, advertising is the iconographic identification of the good with goods. Advertising displays the good as existing in things, in all the things we can use, produce, imagine, buy, consume. Conversely, advertising images always reflect and represent human happiness and human perfection as something embodied in a commodity, or as something that the individual can embody through a special object.

The basis of this identification and therefore of the normative power of images is taste. Recognizing taste, in all its contingency and variability, as the ultimate cause of economic, moral, and aesthetic value, and as the ultimate site for creating such value, advertising transforms socially and collectively consumed images into a huge "organ of collective taste" through which a community selects and builds its own cultural identity and makes collective decisions about its present and its past.[10] The images that dominate public space are not the object but the organ of our collective judgment.

If taste is more important than rationality (or better, than the traditional image of it), that's because unlike traditional norms, which are based on continuity and are supposed to produce continuity, advertising images have to produce change: they are not limited to the actual behavior of consumers—they have to suggest a change in it, and also justify this change. Advertising is the reversal of the traditional customary normativity [*mos*]:[11] if in ancient Rome the goal of the normative system was to stabilize the ancestors' customs, advertising must produce the mobilization of all customs, the customization of all customs. The normativity embodied in advertising produces a constant revolution in customs and habits and coincides with a *mos novissimorum*, a sort of paradoxical tradition (since *mos* means custom and tradition), which has to be constantly renewed, and in which only the drive for newness is stable. It is, in this sense, the exact opposite of censorship in ancient Rome: instead of "punishing novel misdeeds and bringing back the old customs" [*castigare . . . nova flagitia et priscos revocare mores*, Liv. 39,41,4], it pursues the goal of punishing old misdeeds and triggering new customs [*priscos castigare mores et novos advocare habitos*]. Instead of codifying traditional ways of behavior, it must glorify newness. This is also the reason for the predominance of advice over commandment: advertising has to suggest a transformation, and psychology is turned into psychagogy.

Thanks to advertising, our relationship to the world and culture is fundamentally defined by *fashion*: a mobile, ironic,[12] uncertain relationship, a rhythm of change that obliges everyone to revise or discard the old for new elements and forms, which have to be chosen from among different models without any type of objectivity.[13] Advertising, as the specific normative system in which custom can exist only in the form of change, is the transcendental condition of possibility for fashion. This peculiar transformation is what produces the end of cultures in favor of subcultures. One could say that where images and not words are the source of political life there is no more culture (and there could not be a set of cultures), but only subcultures (which, unlike culture, are always chosen, not universal and ephemeral).

WHEN THE EGO IS AN IMAGE—FASHION

There is one sphere that proves that political existence is made possible by images and not by words nowadays (or that political existence is a form of our sensory life and not of our linguistic acts): fashion. Since at least the seventies (think, for instance, of Yves Saint Laurent's *collection scandale* in 1971, or of the invention of the new ready-to-wear brands such as The Gap or Benetton), fashion has no longer been a question of class distinction and of producing prestige, but has rather become an open-air laboratory for the perpetual construction of identities and ways of being—*façonnage de soi* (self-fashioning). This transformation—perhaps the most important moral revolution of the twentieth century—is important for at least two reasons. On the one hand, in this transformation of fashion from an instrument for reproducing social divisions into an art for inventing new identities, a lot of what Foucault would have called technologies of the self (or spiritual exercises) now take place in the medium of clothes, in sensory form: fashion became the heir of ancient moral knowledge. Morality has become a material practice trading in colors, shapes, and forms that are seen as the most direct embodiment of our psychological features. At the threshold of body and soul, a piece of clothing allows feelings and subjective qualities to exist objectively—as images—and, conversely, thanks to the clothing image, the body becomes the immediate theater of the Ego. Through fashion, identity exists as image and not just as an incommunicable property; and conversely, images are no longer purely cognitive or aesthetic but are also moral. The ego exists as an image, and clothes are media for morality: fashion is the sphere in which images become tools for constructing morality—a new form of morality. On the other hand, morality is no longer the site of customs and norms, but is rather the sphere of a perpetual deconstruction of the ethos or of the *Sittlichkeit*. Fashion as morality, which is constantly working against the *mos*, ethos, the custom.

CONCLUSION

In a recent book on the 2008 financial crisis, Arjun Appadurai has proposed to describe the collapse "as a linguistic failure and, more exactly, as the failure of a fissive chain of promises." "What failed in the financial markets in 2007–8 was not any single promise, but the chain of promises created in the derivatives market" because of the "capacity of any derivative to monetize previous promises, without regard to the disposition of the prior promises that are its basis or the future promises that may lie further down the promissory chain." "The derivative . . . uses the means of contract to erode the very basis of contracts since it involves promises that rest on failed promises": the crisis represents the "death of the contract as a foundational moral and social form," "the self-destruction of the contractual form as it comes to cannibalize itself through the form of the credit default swap."[14] This diagnosis is important for two reasons: first, it shows that the crisis of a politics based on contracts—that is, on language—stems not from the weakening or rarefication of words and contracts, but rather from their unchecked multiplication. That's why, instead of calling for a reinstatement of the rule of law, Appadurai evokes "a different conception of the ground from which we can . . . pursue sociality on terms that, in leaving behind both the modern individual and the modern contract, have a reasonable chance of beating global finance at its own game." The problem of contemporary politics is not the anesthetization of words; on the contrary, it is the excess of power that we grant to language, to contracts, to promises. In order to invent a new world, it is necessary to change the ground. This other ground, I think, is the ground produced and offered by images: we already live in another form of political life, which has very little to do with the one invented and formalized by the ancient and modern legal tradition. All we need to do is to recognize it. Advertising and fashion are just the primitive, sometimes grotesque, but ultimately irrepressible prefiguration of the new politics to come.

GOODS

THE LAST NAME OF THE GOOD

They are everywhere, but we are only dimly aware of them. We open our eyes and before us unfurls an endless expanse of commodities. They fill our rooms and our homes. They cover our bodies, outlining silhouettes and identities for each of us. They are what we eat. They are often what we desire. They are what we live among. We move only thanks to them and we live inside of them; often we communicate through them.

Commodities are the flashiest residents of our cities: they reign from those little street temples for hurried passers-by, store windows; they paper the most visible walls of the busiest neighborhoods; they cover every inch of a city's surface, delineating the real boundaries of civilization. It would be difficult to make an exhaustive list of them. The category of "commodity" contains within it the origin, the lifespan, and the fate of nearly all the things with which we directly interact. "Commodity" is the most general and common metaphysical heading for the category of the object, its most commonplace synonym: to come into the world as a thing, to be one of the things of the world, it seems necessary to be or to be capable of becoming a commodity. With only a hint of irony we could say that Heidegger's *in-der-Welt-Sein* amounts to being-among-commodities.

They are everywhere, and yet the word *commodity*, even prior to being an economic or anthropological category, is a defamatory label. We live producing, acquiring, selling, using, imagining, and desiring commodities—but to say that something is a "commodity" seems more like an insult than an objective description. The historical and spiritual reasons for this persistent bad faith are somewhat murky. Still, it seems clear that in communally defining things as commodities we do not describe some real quality of theirs, but rather transform them into moral forces. This is neither a tic of common speech nor a tired but still lingering ideology. Contrary to popular belief, commodities both in theory and in practice have much more to do with morality than with economics. This is the hypothesis from which this book springs: commodities are the extreme form of the good, the most recent name Western culture has given to the good.

This may seem like a paradoxical argument. Instead, it is a banal assertion, one that any one of us could make once we have begun to take seriously the shape of the world we live in. Even more so than textbooks of political economy, sociology, or anthropology, it is the walls of our cities that relentlessly speak to us of commodities, constructing a discourse of words and images about them, explaining to us day after day "what they really are," what they're for, why we need to use them. It is the walls that surround us, not the writings of social scientists, that study and analyze them, one by one. On the city walls, commodities always show up as moral forces, but in the opposite way than we usually think. A commodity is always the presence or sign of a supreme good, the concrete version, as it were, of our happiness. Given the deaf and practically dumb perseverance with which this discourse plasters over every inch of public space, it would be naïve to see it as merely an echo of hegemonic ideology. And even if it were just a pretty lie, schemed up by the elite to dominate and oppress the rest of the population, we would still have to account for this strange form of *Bovarysme* afflicting contemporary metropolises. In fact, our cities talk relentlessly about commodities when they talk about happiness. We are accustomed to thinking about and representing morality and economics as two opposing and irreconcilable spheres; yet they overlap every day, in the singular, uninterrupted discourse that the walls construct before our very eyes.

Rather than denying these facts, or numbering them among the many contradictions of our society, we should give them all the attention they deserve. This book begins with the supposition that it is only possible to understand *what* a commodity is by interrogating the particular site where it becomes recognizable as itself, that is, by examining the place that it occupies in our cities: the walls. It is on the walls of our cities, in fact, that advertisements—commodities' appeals, *la réclame des choses*—most insistently turn up. Only by looking to the walls will we be able to solve the mystery of commodities. Try for just a few moments to suspend judgment, to look around you, observing the walls in a city. You will discover that the relationship between commodities and walls is no accident, and it runs much deeper than one might imagine.

They are not just messages—their contents are both too vague and too broad to be reduced to information. And yet, through the ambiguous, distracted images that make up this enormous open-air atlas, we strain to formulate and communicate knowledge that is urgent and necessary for daily life.

They almost never really contain instructions for use. Sometimes they lack real content; other times, more simply, they talk about things other than their purported content. And what's more, no one, not even the people who make them, really believes what they say. And yet it's almost always their distracted whisper or their mad cry that has suggested to us what we should eat or drink, how we should dress, how to care for our bodies, how to travel, which objects to use.

The knowledge that they transmit is not a spontaneous product of experience. Their rhymes are always the product of calculation, of will, of a real art. And yet their jingles have replaced proverbs in our minds, and survive there like the wisdom of some unlikely, imaginary civilization. The world that they speak of, moreover, does not exist.

Ads rent the fabric of our daily experiences, investing them with parallel lives and prospects. They are habits of the imagination that invite us to let the present world slip a few inches, just enough to let in one extremely powerful and absolutely ordinary object of desire at a time.

The collection of images and words that make up what we call "advertising" is not just the (extreme, perverse) result of a marketing strategy. It's also a kind of laboratory, a place where we expose ourselves daily to the unknown effects that contemplating lives other than our own can have on us. Advertising is a giant experiment of the contemporary collective moral imagination—its biggest, most pervasive, most visible experiment. It's an enormous iconic and conceptual reflection on the world and its components, as well as on human happiness, its forms, and its possibilities. It's an everlasting syllogism that has been unfolding for years in front of the whole world, in all the languages of the world—and it is bold enough (and knowledgeable enough) to address itself to everyone.

The time has come to observe with the necessary curiosity, and without prejudices, this anonymous and contradictory catechism, which, like a rosary symbolically linking all the cities of the new industrial world, allows us to rattle off the most profound, strange prayers and desires that our civilization has been able to formulate. Secular and deeply religious at once, hedonist and ascetic, carnivalesque but also obsessed with discipline, this uninterrupted cosmic litany can reveal much more about the spirit of our epoch than treatises of moral philosophy do.

It teaches us, for example, that the moral imagination often eschews the category of truth and never needs to really believe in what it sees or says to conceive of happiness and the good. If it prefers make-believe and harmless illusions, this is not in order to conceive of reality more clearly or in greater detail, but because its precise object is never (or hardly ever) an action to carry out—rather, it's a different world, a superior, more intense world than the one in which it finds itself. Contemporary moral reflection—at least as practiced covertly by advertising—has nothing to do with norms. It is a pure and extreme form of psychagogy. This is why the divisions proper to other disciplines fall away in this sphere. Science and art, reason and myth, are no longer contradictory poles, but give shape, in advertising, to one homogeneous, indivisible discourse. It's a form of knowledge about life and its forms, which takes the same shape as the life it purports to apply to.

What's more, it teaches us that our most urgent moral concerns are not about enigmatic superhuman divinities, nor about the deepest truths of our unconscious, but about objects, about the things of daily use—a shirt, a telephone, a tie, a ring, a necklace. Advertising morality is dominated by a single, sweet, and desperate obsession: the love for things, for all the things that can be imagined, produced, consumed, or exchanged. If we need to imagine to such an extent and to talk at such lengths about things, this is because we need to express, give shape to, and enable our love for things. The anthropology posited by these truthless moral meditations is different from that assumed by other discourses. The human being sketched in it is neither a speaking animal nor a thinking, living, or producing creature—it is a human being who loves things, who lives by things and for things.

Like every love, this love too has its rules and its whims. And if romantic love is sworn for eternity, the love for things, whose gay science advertising tries to formulate, is rigorously, religiously ephemeral. Its lifespan need not exceed that of a winter or a spring. The deepest reasons for this adherence to transience are hard to understand. But it would be naïve to see this as a sign of weakness or failure: it takes much more strength and discipline to constantly change one's object of desire than to concentrate upon a single beloved. In straining to constantly love new objects, the society that lives according to this new morality is forced to periodically reconstruct the world of things with which it surrounds itself—it is obligated, with every new season, to give new shape to the materials in which it embodies itself, to reimagine the objects through which it constructs its own identity. And there's something poetic, even noble, in this inhuman struggle, like that of a phoenix determined to be reborn from its own ashes and, at the end of every summer, to question once more all the certainties by which it lived. If the apocalypse is one of the most common ways of collectively imagining the future, this is because at the end of each season we burn all the things that we had erected to give shape to our world.

In the end, the morality whispered by our city walls provides an important clue about the shape of the world we live in. Advertising is a discourse about things, the forms they take, their very being. This discourse is, however, different from the one produced by other forms of knowledge about things, such as physics, chemistry, or engineering. In this form of knowledge-become-public, things are no longer recognizable as more or less stable states of aggregation of matter. In advertising, every object is simply the form that matter assumes every time it comes into contact with human experience; in this encounter, however, the stakes are no longer technical or physical, but rather purely moral. If things have become the center of ethical reflection, this is because the material world itself has ceased to be either a mere physical extension or a purely physical phenomenon. In the most widespread, common discourse attempting to describe its features, the material world today characterizes itself in the first place as a moral phenomenon, not a physical one—as the metaphysical site where good and bad are defined. Some people acquire and collect objects in order to attain a crumb (or a simulacrum) of happiness, while others condemn the universe of commodities as the ultimate source of inauthenticity in our times; some make saving the material world—nature—the most urgent political task of our time, and see respecting the environment (the balance of the material world) as the highest moral duty; and others, in dreaming of a more just world, can only describe the future lives they imagine by relating them to the material world in all its forms (food, technology, energy). But every time that we talk about morality, we are talking in one way or another about the material world. And vice versa, what once upon a time was the natural sciences' chosen object of inquiry now obsesses those who seek to understand what is good and what is bad.

1

WALLS

I'm astonished, wall, that you haven't collapsed into ruins,
since you're holding up the weary verse of so many poets.
—ON THE WALLS OF POMPEII [CIL IV, 2487]

The oldest human things of which evidence remains are stones. It was
through stones, in fact, that human intelligence issued forth from interiority and consciousness, embodying itself in the world of things. Used,
worked, or sculpted, stone is the primordial object—the oldest vehicle of the
human spirit and the first form of culture. It was out of and with stones that
man built his first instruments, the first things used to make other things.
Stones are not only the foundation of culture, but also the archetype of
every form of technology.[1] In a metaphysical paradox that has yet to be the-
orized, it's our relation to the universe's most solid, remote material that
furnishes evidence of human intelligence's greatest transformations, indel-
ibly recording our progress, measuring the history of our species. There is
a mineralogy of the spirit still waiting to be written.

To the self-consciousness of modern man, the "Stone Age" connotes a
distant epoch, one that may never have existed—and yet, we have never
really left it. It is still through stone that we give shape to space, and it is
thanks to stone that we can define our social and political existence. Still
today, the city remains a "thing of stone": an orderly gathering of walls, a
collection of lives enclosed by stones. And it is still walls—that is, stone
things—that determine the dimensions of our cities, define the layout of
streets, and separate public from private space.

However, if stone is the political "thing" par excellence—the raw material of our entire social existence—this is not simply because it allows us to divide up and delimit communal space. When we conceive of the wall as the basic form of any political space, we are referring to its ability to produce enclaves. In other words, we are thinking of the fact that the wall perfectly embodies the mechanism of exclusion and inclusion that seems to be the founding act of any political community. And yet, with the same gesture by which every wall separates and molds spaces, it also creates surfaces on which the community sketches its own portrait. Without these surfaces, no city could exist: this is the first concrete space in which the communal reveals itself in tangible form—the first objective site of the *partage du sensible* (distribution of the sensible). On the walls, spiritual life and material life become inseparable, as stone masonry unites symbol and nature. This is why a city is never a mere archipelago of *enclaves*: it is above all a being of surfaces that won't stop making itself seen, communicating its own image,[2] and talking about itself.

On stone, man promptly learned to draw—to represent reality, to share his ideas and his dreams with everyone else. Walls do not simply define the borders of places in space—they also embody the memory and self-consciousness of a place. Still today they symbolize public space par excellence, the surface upon which the city and the individual have recorded their knowledge, norms, and judgments.

It was on the expanses of city walls—vertical, solid, public, universally visible—that power began to inscribe its word: laws were first published on city walls. For centuries, it was on this very surface that we stored measurements, prices, and commercial regulations.[3]

It was on city walls that solar and astronomical time became measurable; and it was on walls that the memory of time past—the names of the dead, their last words—was always preserved. The same "thing" that allowed both ancient and modern cities to take on shape and existence has always also been used to record their history, to glorify heroes, to recite the rosary of the names of power, and to paint each portrait in the spinning wheel of emperors, rulers, kings, and gods.

On stone walls, however, we preserve not only official, eloquent, or authoritative writings but also public moods and individual opinions; graffiti registering protests, tributes, or rebellion; and songs and praises. This is illustrated by Pompeii's graffiti, which Lombroso termed the "true tattoos of the walls"[4]—as well as by the walls of men's bathrooms across Europe,[5] or of teenagers' rooms, which are literally frescoed with pictures of new heroes and their words. It was on city walls that the Paris uprising of May '68 delivered its most lasting messages, and it is on city walls that Banksy, Blu, Alexandre Farto, and other street artists create their works.

In reality, city walls have always been a space for projection and a space for manufacturing phantasmagoria. It was to the internal walls of its churches that Christian civilization commended its dreams, utopias, and nightmares. The frescoes of Europe's cathedrals enabled the Christian pantheon to occupy public space. And this storytelling-in-stone was not just the prerogative of religious space. In aristocratic palaces, ancient courts, and royal estates, too, walls hosted the mythology of the past and the celebration of one's own power. And we continue to project our most secret dreams, now not inside churches, but rather in the cinema—in the dark interiors of theaters where each one of us, together with a thousand others, abandons herself to daydreaming. If the wall is, among things, the "political thing" par excellence, this is because it teaches us that every city is not just a space of cohabitation, but more especially a space of shared imaginative projection. A city does not simply need walls to protect itself; it needs them to talk about itself, its history, and its happiness. A city becomes self-conscious via the same material that composes it: it reflects on how it is formed of people and things. More than a mere thing, it is simultaneously a reflection upon itself; and the city wall is the thing that enables this simultaneity.

It is as if, thanks to the walls, every city had two bodies, a "mineral" one that takes up space and gives it shape, and a semiotic or symbolic one that only exists on the surface of the first one and has a dream-like texture. These two bodies overlap, but never perfectly correspond.[6] And this second body is like an immense, collective stone organ, capable of infinitely multiplying experiences, of transforming a city into a kaleidoscope of images, feelings, and signs—but also of recording everything we think or say.[7] It enhances our senses, like a prosthesis. Thanks to its walls, a city becomes an internal sense organ that produces and stores communal feelings and thoughts.[8]

This is why the stone inscriptions of every age constitute a kind of spiritual tattoo, the first signs a population uses to reflect upon its existence. They are the first tangible—and certainly the longest lasting—incarnation of what modern political philosophy has called the public sphere.[9] And the images, faces, and words that comprise this spatialized symbolic order express the collective ethos of the city—what Hegel would have called *Sittlichkeit*, its concrete morality. It was here that every citizen learned shared political know-how, public rules, universally acknowledged civic values—in short, the axiology of the polis. In this same space, the shared moral and political gaze took shape. The public good became a visible thing on the walls, a tangible reality—above all, an image or a word shared materially, not just spiritually. This is why city walls have always been so important. And this is why, if we really want to understand who we are, we must again start reading the walls. It's on the walls that the historian must seek the face of the city again and again. The spirit of a civilization is above all an epigraphic phenomenon: it is stored in stone in a more immediate and lasting way than it is in human consciousness.

Epigraphy, the science of wall writing, teaches us that in the past, communication effected in stone—on a kind of open-air, public page—had primarily to do with three spheres. First, that of politics, the state, its men, and their careers—where a city glorified itself, its own heroes, and its own history; next, that of religion, with the representation and celebration of gods and demigods; and finally, that of funerary culture, the province of the cult of the dead. This was a monumental body of literature and iconography that, from a rhetorical point of view, had specific characteristics: its language was formulaic, repetitive, and concise, and the *ductus* was mostly nominal; its message was stylized, and the scenes it depicted were highly conventional. And thanks to epigraphy, we also know that emperors and rulers always conceived of this space as the medium of a global strategy of communication, which allowed the very state to conceive of itself differently and allowed the citizens to conceptualize, know, and *see* public affairs.[10]

Politics, Aristotle wrote at the beginning of his *Nicomachean Ethics*, is the supreme form of architecture:[11] ancient culture and political science often equated legislation with the construction of the perimeter of walls protecting the city—or with the walls of the temple at the center of its spiritual life.[12] Walls have always been the natural element from which cities are made, but they are also their alphabet and voice, the chief organ that lets them speak. Even today our cities are an intarsia of interlocking walls. And even today, that space is put to good use—penciled with writings, images, and symbols. Of course, since Aloys Senefelder invented the lithograph in 1797, the majority of urban epigraphic texts are no longer carved in stone but rather, through stone (Solnhofen limestone), printed on paper, and then, often, hung once more on stone. The new urban tattoos have a different name, and to produce them, a succession of different techniques has been employed—and yet, the walls remain spaces of projection and collective imagination. What has changed, however, are the subjects of this commemorative literature. The same symbolic spaces that were used in ancient times to honor and sanctify the gods, the city, and the dead—that is, epigraphic and architectural monuments—are today home to a discourse that incessantly talks about and displays *things*—celebrating, glorifying, and exalting them. Our cities have been abandoned by the gods—they no longer erect monuments to publicly recognized heroes—but they have been invaded by images of the most diverse objects of daily use: shampoos, telephones, perfumes, records, bras, shoes, chocolate, meat—all the things that, simply, we call commodities.

If the Romans used stone to celebrate their own victories (one might think, for example, of Trajan's column), a Parisian can see on the walls of her own city enormous oversized posters of steak cutlets: "*Chronoviande*: buy meat in one click," one could read recently on the underground walls of the Paris metro. If we go beyond the surrealism inherent in such a substitution, epigraphy shows us that advertising, a phenomenon generally considered to be categorically modern, is in fact part of a much older tradition. Advertising is but the transformation, on the level of content much more than of nature or form, of that "morality in stone" that has always structured our cities. "Morality" should be understood here in the classical and literal sense of the word: the city has always incorporated on its walls a science of the good and the bad—a body of knowledge that orients our choices and defines our customs, because it shows what is good and what should be imitated or desired.

Contrary to what we generally think, however, this relentless, blind communication is not the destruction of morality: at least from a structural and formal point of view, it is quite simply morality embodied in objects other than the traditional ones. In reality, substituting the representation of all kinds of commodities for the representation of an imaginary deity, winged beings, or celebrated battles (or massacres) glorifying a dead civilization is not particularly alienating or morally indecent. In fact, there's something undeniably lyrical about this transformation. Imagine if a contemporary metropolis were buried under the ashes and dust of a volcanic eruption, such that, like Pompeii, it were preserved for centuries in its current state. A few centuries from now, archeologists discovering this city would find themselves confronted with something extremely mysterious: a civilization literally obsessed with things, to the point that it devoted practically all the public discourse and architectural symbolism structuring their towns to things.

In contemporary discussions of capitalism—its origins, history, and aporias—there has been a great deal of reflection on the anthropological premises of our civilization. We never tire of pointing out that the world that we live in is the result of a few fundamental passions: interest, the desire for accumulation, greed.[13] It has been repeatedly observed that technology was essential in accelerating production and intensifying exchange and consumption; the inequality between workers and bourgeoisie that capitalism tends to produce has been rightly denounced. This is all true— but it risks masking a more commonplace but equally undeniable fact: that the civilization we live in has produced objects that, in their variety and quantity, have no equivalent in history—and that it has invested lowly, ordinary objects with a value and a care for design or manufacture that is equally incomparable. Gods are not born, heroes are not to be found. But periodically we fete the appearance of new cars, collections of clothing, telephones, furniture, or computers. We dedicate nearly all of our time, energy, and love to dreaming up, manufacturing, distributing, and consuming these objects. And above all, the civilization we live in has invested things and commodities with that public form of storytelling, midway between mythology and morality, that other civilizations directed either to the sky or to their own history. The city itself is for all of us first and foremost a body tattooed with images and writings, with small and large narratives, at whose center the good is always—and exclusively—incarnated as one thing: the commodity. Conversely, advertising is the site at which things offer themselves to everyone's gaze, becoming the object of an open-air phantasmagoria, and above all inhabiting a space that, morally, is not insignificant. On the walls, commodities pass from the condition of being an object of production, distribution, and private consumption to that of being a publicly perceived symbol—or better, of being a *good* that everyone comes to know. It is important to reflect on the profound historical, structural, and rhetorical continuity between advertising and public epigraphic communication because that allows us to better understand what makes an object into a commodity. We will only be able to understand the nature of commodities and their value in our civilization by reflecting on the fact that, thanks to advertising, the citizen actually encounters the commodity in the political space where the city has always articulated and portrayed its own ethos. When they talk about the good and about happiness, today our cities always and only talk to us about commodities: the good that we never quit talking about in cities is goods, merchandise. And conversely, the commodity is the only form in which the good is publicly thinkable and articulable today.

2

CITIES

The Metropolis today is a classroom; the ads are its teachers.
— MARSHALL McLUHAN

"The city," wrote one of the fathers of American sociology, "is something more than a congeries of individual men and of social conveniences—streets, buildings, electric lights, tramways, and telephones, etc.; something more, also, than a mere constellation of institutions and administrative devices—courts, hospitals, schools, police, and civil functionaries of various sorts. The city is, rather, a state of mind."[1] This "state of mind" does not hover above material structures like an intangible ether; on the contrary, it dwells in stone—it is its very voice. Every single thing in the city is to some extent a state of mind, because in the city even the stones speak. What we call a city is, at root, nothing more than the metaphysical space in which men and stones seem to exchange features with one another. In fact, according to an ancient tradition, citizens are "living stones" [*lithoi zontes*][2]—they are themselves buildings, living edifices, the real body of the city. But that same movement that turns men into stones also turns stones into spirit, into the "mineral mind" of the community. A city is, literally, the place where stones acquire that most human of faculties, the song [*saxa loquuntur*]:[3] a city's stones, as we have seen, praise its history, display its gods, dictate its laws, and reproduce the city in its own image—to put it more prosaically, they speak to us of the things of daily life, of commodities.

This is not just a projection: the symbolism of the city is not only the result of images and words that stone collects on its own surface, and the song of stone is not limited to epigraphic writing. Just by means of their shape, buildings "speak," and in their very function they are speaking symbols, like any artifact.[4] The most paradoxical form of this is what historians of architecture have called the "duck," that type of building whose very form recalls its function.[5] In such buildings, sculpture and architecture, function and symbol seem to blend into one another. And neither in this case is this a modern phenomenon: the cross-shaped plan of churches and cathedrals answers to this very same need.[6] But apart from such "representational" extremes, every architectural work participates in a discourse that includes all of a city's constructions, even the most minimalist ones. Architecture is always the organ of a collective dream; what Walter Benjamin wrote about Hausmann's Paris—that it was a "phantasmagoria rendered in stone"[7]—can in fact be extended to every other modern city. Every urban space is imagination transferred onto stone, or, one might say, the dream shared by walls and stone. And if a society is, as Mauss wrote, largely a by-product of its symbolism, this is because the space constituted by stones, walls, and buildings is the first dream-like objectification of this very symbolism—stone is the privileged organ of every society's collective symbolism. "City" is, at its root, the word that we have for millennia given not to a more or less sizeable collection of humans (i.e., a society), but rather to the space in which things exist in the way that humans exist. If politics is the supreme form of architecture, this is because it's the mechanism that allows stones and things to sing.

Advertising is thus not just the contemporary form of that epigraphic communication that has always existed in the city. It is the continuation and specialization of that *natural* public symbolism of which the walls have always been the collective organs. In fact, even just from a strictly quantitative point of view it would be difficult to ascribe a quality of parasitism to the relationship between advertising and the urban landscape. The panoply of advertising devices of all shapes and sizes is by now a characteristic feature of our cities' personalities; it is difficult to think about New York, London, Tokyo—about their allure and their beauty—without imagining the electric advertising *pinacothèques* that sit in state in Times Square, Piccadilly Circus, or Shibuya. "To deprive the city of them would be like depriving San Gimignano of its towers or the City of London of its Wren steeples."[8] But from a historical point of view, too, advertising is equally hard to think of as a complementary, secondary, or accessory component of urban space. Historians of contemporary architecture have repeatedly reminded us that advertising structures (whether signs, posters, or electronic billboards) extend one of the classic forms of architectonic construction: that which privileges symbol over form, communicating over structuring space.[9] This is the very same process that was at work in the construction of any given Gothic or Baroque cathedral facade.[10] And just as in the case of the billboard, once architecture is relieved of the task of giving shape to space, it invents antispatial techniques—it becomes purely a matter of symbols, confronting issues of style, decoration, and surface. Just like advertising structures, here too, "architecture in this landscape becomes symbol in space rather than form in space."[11] Such architectonic genres are characterized by a certain illusionism. The trompe-l'oeil so characteristic of advertising posters is the direct descendant of the baroque cathedral facade, "bigger in scale and higher outside than inside."[12]

The link between a lush swath of advertising and industrial symbols, like the Strip in Las Vegas, and the oldest Gothic, Eclectic, or Romantic buildings is not just rhetorical—culturally, it's much deeper than that. In reality, both are forms of popular and vernacular construction. Contrary to what we tend to think, the preeminence of the symbol over space does not issue from refined or erudite architecture—rather, like in other artistic and literary genres, it is the mark of the humblest styles. It's hardly necessary to harken all the way back to the romantic mythologies that taught us to see figurative art and allegory as the genuine mode of expression of primitive populations, or of those that are closest to nature. It was Pop Art, with its use of brands and commercial symbols, that revealed the forest of billboards that has sprung up in our cities as the direct expression of a kind of "folklore of industrial man" (to cite the title of Marshall McLuhan's famous work,[13] which came out at the very moment of Pop Art's birth) and not as a mere symptom or tool of some sort of cultural hegemony.

Even when analyzed through the lens of a history of architectural styles, the iconography of commercial advertising constitutes more the *sermo humilis* of local vernacular[14] than a cultured and "culturalized" reworking. We have to relearn to see in urban advertising formulas the degree zero of symbolism (architectural and otherwise), which is the mark of all the popular arts.[15] If these latter are more valuable in the eyes of a historian, that's because they often reflect, without mediation, the spirit of an age, rather than the personality and idiosyncrasies of the artist.[16] This is why the "folklore of advertising" is a particularly significant expression of our time, even when it's produced by skilled professionals (as all the arts are, according to etymological evidence even prior to anthropological evidence). Of course, the "folklore of industrial man," McLuhan wrote, "stems from the laboratory, the studio, and the advertising agencies. But amid the diversity of our inventions and abstract techniques of production and distribution there will be found a great degree of cohesion and unity. This consistency is not conscious in origin or effect and seems to arise from a sort of collective dream."[17] We need to understand the nature of this collective dream about things and their value that is advertising—because only in it, and not just in the real order of transactions and exchanges, or in statistics about production and consumption, can we discover the face of that utopian norm of existence and the world that we call economics.

The analysis of both epigraphic and other kinds of urban symbolism has enabled us to arrive at important conclusions. We have learned, first of all, that advertising is not an extraneous and parasitical element that has invaded our cities. It is the most diffuse vernacular form of the symbolism that defines the state of existence of everything in a city. This means, for one thing, that it cannot be viewed as a natural consequence of the market or an invention of late capitalism. Advertising is not the soul of the market, but one of the infinite voices of the city. Or better: it is the main dialect spoken by stones today.

We have learned, too, that through advertising the contemporary city recuperates the premodern iconographic tradition—in which painting, sculpture, design, and music were combined with architecture—and makes of the city a kind of total work of art. It does this, however, not to invite us to imagine a God, legions of winged beings, or flanks of virtuous men, but rather to present commodities as moral forces—not as simple products, but rather as fragments of the good in which we should participate. A church was an incredible architectonic machine, in which space became a moral symbol, and stone had above all to incarnate and represent a moral order. The contemporary city is an immense open-air cathedral, completely frescoed and literally plastered with certain structures of a liturgical origin, which were originally tied to a cult and to sacred space, and which are very similar to the altars of a medieval cathedral—namely, store windows. Stores—those little temples in which the light never goes out, as if they sheltered the sacred fire of Vesta—are the expression and symptom (but not the cause) of the fact that with things, or better with certain things—commodities—we maintain a relationship that is anything but purely economic or commercial. We adore things; we venerate them as if they were relics; we consider them, quite rightly, to be our most concrete means of attaining happiness.

All this should lead us to think about the relationship between advertising and commodities in a new way. We tend to think of advertising as a side effect of commodity production and its excesses, or as the tool of those who want to foster consumption. What we have seen thus far, however, should have demonstrated that it is impossible to view the relation between commodity and advertising as one of cause and effect. Just as the city is not chronologically anterior to the symbolism of which it is object and which it itself practices, so too the commodity is not ontologically or chronologically prior to advertising. On the contrary, advertising would seem to be something immediately and intrinsically linked to the commodity's existence: it is in the nature of things to be talked about in the city. And vice versa, precisely because there can be no commodity without advertising (that is, without that sort of collective dream which intensifies them in the form of symbols), the life of commodities is intrinsically political and cannot be a simple economic or individual fact.

In fact, seen from this vantage point, even what, following Marx, we generally call "commodity fetishism" seems to lose the teleological and ideological traits that we have wanted at all costs to ascribe to it.[18] The market is not responsible for the fact that commodities—the things we use in the city, and constantly desire, manufacture, distribute, and consume; the things we constantly talk about—always represent something more than their simple use. "Capitalism" is not what transforms objects into "sensuous things which are at the same time suprasensible or social," laden with a value and symbolism in no way inferable from their nature.[19] This is because it is not thanks to production—that is, to the process by which the communal social substance called "work" is deposited and crystallized in things—that commodities acquire a social form. Speech, or symbolism, is the original and primordial state of all the things in the city. In other words, fetishism is a political phenomenon, not an economic one. Of course, commodities speak—but they speak in exactly the same way as all stones in a city do. And of course, commodities speak, but they don't limit themselves to "reflect[ing] the social characteristics of men's own labor as objective characteristics of the products of labour themselves."[20] If commodities speak, giving life to a "system of signs," that's because in a city everything is a symbol as well as a reality, and everything has a public image, at once dreamlike and shared.[21] Politics, it has been said, is nothing more than the technique of extracting from each thing, even from a stone, something more than its simple use value—of transforming stone into symbol, and symbol into stone. The dual nature that we so often assume to be a specific feature of the commodity is in fact the nature of every wall. Every wall is in reality "a very strange thing, abounding in metaphysical subtleties and theological niceties."[22] And, beyond its use value (that of producing enclaves, of giving shape to space), every wall has a symbolic value that comes into tension with its other kind of value.

If commodities and advertising are a naturally political phenomenon, this is because a city is a place where one speaks of things, and at the same time it is the metaphysical space where things can speak. What's more, in advertising, it is as if urban symbolism is brought to its logical conclusion. It is only thanks to advertising that absolutely *everything* speaks—even the most ordinary things. Not only gods and ancient heroes, but also bras, shoes, cars. Everything gains a voice.

3

THE BANALITY OF THE GOOD

Ich weiß nicht, was soll es bedeuten,
Daß ich so traurig bin,
Ein Märchen aus uralten Zeiten,
Das kommt mir nicht as dem Sinn.

—HEINRICH HEINE, "DIE LORELEI"[1]

If the walls of our cities are plastered with images of things, this is never for purely decorative reasons: the symbolism proper to every city, even advertising symbolism, is never just aesthetic. The collection of symbols and emblems that are sedimented in stone or that shape stone answers to the same need that brought about the invention of road signs. We need signs and symbols because our existence in the city is only possible through them. Only thanks to this primordial symbolism, in fact, do we learn to orient ourselves, and only in this symbolic space does every resident know the city: she learns the name of streets, memorizes their twists and turns, understands the purpose and function of each building, constructs an image of the place where she lives. But if urban symbolism cannot be reduced to a system of road signs or a collection of retail signs, that's because the orientation that every resident needs is not simply physical or geographical, but more especially moral and political. This is ultimately the reason this "second skin" exists: it is not merely a city's external trappings, but the stuff of a real branch of public knowledge. In fact, it constitutes public knowledge par excellence. At bottom, even before it becomes an object of study for an elite group of specialists, every city features a local knowledge base, a kind of indigenous sociology or anthropology available to all its residents, which has been sedimented in a thousand different forms on its surface.[2] From this point of view, every city is an open-air theater that perennially stages a show of itself, its image, and its forms. What we call culture is also the collection of these representations.

Connecting advertising back to its epigraphic origins and to the broadest and deepest forms of urban symbolism—of which, as we have seen, it is a dialect and variation—means not simply freeing it from the orbit of pure ideology or commercial strategy, but moreover recognizing it as a form of knowledge. Advertising is the one form of discourse about happiness and the perfection of human life that's allowed in—and spread throughout—our cities. But it is also a kind of indigenous anthropology of contemporary cities.[3] Through advertising, in effect, a whole society expresses and praises not only its totem objects, but more especially the lifestyles, emotions, and habits that are meant at every turn to be taken as moral and anthropological exemplars.

We must begin to interrogate this huge, absolute discourse that every urban society produces about itself without contempt, and not just through the lens of aesthetics or semiotics. If it merits the title of "absolute discourse," this is first of all because it shapes the city, insofar as it is the most widespread and common idiolect of urban symbolism. It is also "absolute" in the sense that, unlike other forms of symbolism proper to our culture (from literature and movies to sculpture and theater), it is able to simultaneously inhabit the totality of public and private media that we use to communicate and to make use of every language and style of our culture—to pass through every substrate and superficial layer. Advertising, at its core, is the most supple and communicable form of moral knowledge that we possess; what distinguishes it from all other forms of moral symbolism and knowledge, which are intrinsically linked to a medium and a specific form, is that advertising can transmigrate from medium to medium, and do so *salva veritate*.[4] A road or retail sign loses its meaning if it is moved from the wall to a newspaper or the television. A novel shifts in nature when it passes from printed page to silver screen. An ad, on the other hand, seems capable of passing from one medium to another without experiencing any damage to its contents, or any loss of its semantic value. In its ease of mobility, advertising is the perfect instance of that "migration of symbols"[5] that has preoccupied art history for so long.[6]

If advertising appears to be an absolute discourse, this is above all because it internalizes and displays all the ways of life, habits, and savoir faire of contemporary man, recording all the things of our world, calling them by their names—and it does so with the greatest possible precision: it does not talk in general about skirts or shoes, but about *this* skirt and *this* shoe. It is, in essence, a kind of immense, open-air atlas, an inventory of all the possible illustrations of collective memory and public imagination—an archive that's much more exhaustive than the walls of cathedrals or the epigraphic writings of antiquity ever were. In this archive, the most disparate elements are connected to one another, as men, natural objects, events, and nonhuman and nonnatural things suddenly find themselves on the same symbolic plane, one where traits pass back and forth between one class and another. This cosmological universalism—the ability to link feelings to things, to link emotions or customs to the most banal objects of experience, to link a collection of meanings to forms of appearance—makes advertising much more detailed and efficient than nearly any other moral discourse. The essayistic tradition focuses on the anatomy of moral existence: it illustrates the physiology of choice, explains the dynamics of decisions, or interrogates the ontology of the good. The novel, that great moral school of modernity,[7] is certainly the best form for grasping the temporality of human existence and for depicting characters, emotions, and the power of interpersonal relationships.[8] Advertising, however, sets next to this reflection on customs, styles, and individuation a theory of all the things of this world and their use. It is a form of collective pedagogy, but it does not only operate through reflection and introspection. It is put into immediate practice in a material way—it is actualized by a world populated by objects as well as by states of mind.

Social fashioning is no longer just a matter of temperaments and attitudes, but more especially of little portable worlds. It's probably this extreme realism that has made advertising the most wide-ranging and influential moral agent in the world.[9] In advertising, morality ceases to be a doctrine of man and his states of mind and becomes a universal doctrine of man's relation to things and the world—a kind of practical cosmology that is made and unmade daily, every time that we desire, imagine, produce, buy, or sell commodities.

When we talk about it, we don't bother to define it. Whether referring to an object, a person, or public life, the good seems to be a given, almost as if it were synonymous with the way things are or as if it were the expression of their truer, more perfect side. And yet the use of this term is not at all clear, even in philosophy. According to traditional genealogies, it is to the sophists that we are indebted for its introduction into philosophy. And legend has it that it was Socrates, the most enigmatic and refined of the sophists, and also the most ambiguous and dangerous among them (the only one who reduced Parmenides to aporia, but also the only one to be put to death), who transformed this word into a weapon that definitively "brought down philosophy from the heavens, placed it in cities, introduced it into families, and obliged it to examine into life and morals, and good and evil,"[10] "disregarding the physical universe and confining his study to moral questions."[11]

On Socrates's lips, the "good" does not refer to a practical, moral phenomenon; perfection and truth are not, in fact, human prerogatives. Everything that exists and is participates in perfection, virtue, and truth—and certainly no thanks to man. It's not easy to define the nature of the good, and Socrates prefers to provide an indirect definition, based on its fruits: the sun is "in the visible world, in relation to sight and the things of sight, what the good is in the intellectual world in relation to mind and the things of mind."[12] And yet it is not a force that operates solely in the domain of the mind:[13] "the good may be said to be not only the author of knowledge to all things known, but of their being and essence."[14] It is through the good, what's more, that "all other things become useful and advantageous."[15] The source of the perfection, virtue, and truth of all things has nothing human about it, but neither can it be equated to one of the things of this world: if everything that is participates in it, this is only because the good "is not essence, but far exceeds essence in dignity and power."[16] The perfection of things, their virtue, has a single cause; but the universality of this source—of the fact that for every single thing it is possible to be good—cannot but be distinct from all other things. The price of the unity of the good is its separateness.

Conversely, precisely because it is separate and abstract, the good is communicable to everything—it is, in fact, the very definition of the communicable. In its perfection, in being good, everything will express something more than its own nature—a completely communal quality, in which all things participate insofar as they are perfect, good, and true. The good is an ecstatic dimension, which takes things beyond their own nature; but in this ecstasy, everything communes with the perfection and truth of all things. From this perspective, human happiness, understood as perfection, has nothing specifically human about it—it is participation in cosmic perfection. When we conceive of happiness as an ecstatic epiphany, as the great novelists of the last few centuries taught us to do, we are simply extending a thought that is Platonic in origin. Catching hold of happiness means grasping that point at which all things accord with one another. This is why the good also represents the apex of political knowledge, indeed of absolute knowledge (*megiston mathema*)[17]—what the philosopher, as guardian of the city, must possess to ensure adequate government—at heart identical to the technical or artistic knowledge from which all things spring.

Conceiving of the good as a cosmic dimension shared by all things allows us to rediscover the unity of the world in this perfection, but it also threatens to make happiness hopelessly unattainable. If the source of the perfection and virtue of things is separate, it will be out of man's reach, impossible to conceive of as "those goods which are practicable and attainable."[18] If it can be said to exist, our perfection would have to be something within our power [*eph'hemin*], something that can be built out of the fabric of reality, out of time, care, and the gestures by which man relates to himself to make and unmake himself and his world: action. If there is anything that gives perfection to our lives, if there is a source of virtue for human life, then it must exist in praxis—it must be something reachable by means of the relation that each man has to his own actions and to himself. It was Aristotle who first conceived of the identity among the good, happiness, and praxis. It was he who objected to Plato that the good for man is by definition a practical dimension, and who discovered, vice versa, that action is the privileged means by which man can obtain the good proper to him—can become perfect, can be happy. "Practical philosophy" is just the perspective that conceives of the *good* as something that man can obtain by means of and in the midst of action.

In this sense, a thing's relation or (more fundamentally) a man's relation to his own good no longer inflects being, but rather doing or acting. While not losing its transcendence with respect to things, the good now designates a space of interiority; in other words, defining *good* as the form and perfection of an object means creating and opening up a space in it for the articulation of a dialectic—a space in which interiority and transcendence are articulated. As Plotinus wrote, the good in this sense means the strength of what is fitting, or what is fitting as strength.[19] Virtuous action is the site where everything suspends or temporarily reduces the exteriority of its own perfection; this is why "the least alloyed and nearest to the good are most at peace within themselves." Praxis is nothing more than "the reconciliation of a thing with its own essence."[20]

Whether as an otherworldly principle that can render all things true and good, or a web of actions thanks to which we manage to acquire perfection and virtue, it seems that the good always exists for us and for the world in the form of a relation to something else. It never appears as the simple congruence of an essence with itself; the good always produces a vibration of its own identity. It is as if, in this world, the union of being and goodness always took the form of their disunion: if things and men are good in the very fact of being, they will be so just to the degree that they do not entirely coincide with the good (the good proper to them)—that is, provided that they maintain a separation between their being and being one's proper good;[21] it doesn't matter whether this space is filled by a relation to a first principle, by action, or by something else. Conceiving of the good means conceiving of a fissure at the heart of all things, between the identity of something and its perfection. What we call ethics is nothing more than the healing of this division internal to each thing, or the (more or less dangerous) equation that can define its identity. It's a question of understanding, in every case, what it is that will make possible an essence's reconciliation with its own perfection.

Since the industrial revolution, we have been getting used to the idea that the metaphysical space by means of which we can enter into relation with the good, in all its forms, is the sphere of the infinite relationships possible with the things that we produce, exchange, imagine, and desire.[22] It is in a relation to commodities—to goods par excellence, to good things, invested with value—that the relation to a possible perfection exists. It is this, fundamentally, that advertising constantly trumpets in all the cities of the Western world. This message can be annoying, but there is something necessary in it, and something undeniably positive. Our society is irreparably and definitively secularized; it has accepted once and for all the death of God; it lives in a cosmos where nature expresses no eternal, immutable, virtuous order that can build a model for praxis, as it could for the ancients. And because of more recent wounds, which our memory has not yet erased, it can no longer believe that the good emerges from the fabric of human actions in time—that is, from history. In such a historical and metaphysical framework, conceiving of the good means conceiving of it as something different from otherworldly phenomena (even just as objects of contemplation)— but also as having nothing to do with praxis and human action. If the good exists, it can only be the object of production. Detached alike from contemplation and from praxis, the good *can only exist as a thing*. The "good" that commodities bring into existence is not divine, but neither is it truly human. It is not natural, but neither does it exist outside the world. On the contrary, it establishes an order for the world, a kind of ever-shifting cosmology, constantly redrawn by commerce and fashion. Advertising, from this point of view, is the first embryonic formulation of morality, once we have accepted the fact that man's fate is a life among things, and that this life among things cannot be transcended—*ever*. Commodities are the extracorporeal organs through which we perceive and breathe the good—a kind of moral life that exists outside of us.

Suddenly, our happiness seems within reach—right here in front of us, separated only by a thin pane of glass. We no longer have to leave the city to find it; we need not exile ourselves in the desert to rehabilitate our desires. No badly dressed priests or stern shamans will show us the way, and struggling to decipher ancient, inscrutable books will be futile. That good which for centuries we have considered unthinkable, unsayable, or unimaginable is a constant and quotidian presence, visible in the most ordinary objects. The good is no longer outside of things—it is ubiquitous, universal, protean. It no longer demands that we search for it; it shows itself, appearing everywhere and in the most diverse forms. The extreme realism of the morality of advertising equates to an idea of the good so shape-shifting that it can encompass practically all things: ads transform commodities into the supreme good and, above all, succeed at calling practically all the things we can experience "commodities." It's as if, in advertising discourse, any phenomenon, regardless of its nature, can for at least a moment aspire to this title, can become a complex of possible happiness—not just an object of value, but a moral source of perfection for any one of us. The mystery of advertising is not just the mystery of a symbolism that involves the entire cosmos without distinguishing between nature and culture, human and nonhuman, or dream and reality. It is above all the mystery of being the site in which an idea of the good completely unlike any of the ideas so laboriously catalogued by Western moral philosophy and theology over the course of the centuries appears and is articulated. The good that cities talk about no longer has divine or otherworldly features, nor is it a practical attribute—it's not an aspect of this or that action, and we do not only experience it when we make a decision. It's ubiquitous, accompanying *all* the gestures and *all* the day-to-day affairs of each of us—a quality proper to all worldly experiences. If the good is something present and real, it is so only thanks to the objects that surround us. The good, happiness, is in things. In *all* things. This is the dream of every city, the morality that each city learns today from its walls: the *good*, in the most proper sense of the term, is by nature more universal than we ever imagined, and it exists in paradoxical form. A television, some chocolate, a shirt: suddenly it is all things that are the site and form of the good and the happiness we seek. This is why economics or semiotics alone cannot solve the puzzle of this modern variation of urban symbolism. If stones sing and speak only of things, that's because we think about and desire the good only in things. We are only happy in cities because the good is now made of the same stuff as stones.

Of course, advertising pursues us relentlessly: it appears everywhere, and it can live on any surface. It is an absolute discourse, capable of cataloguing all the actions and things we experience. And it is a universal discourse, capable of addressing anyone, not just an elite. But its pliability, its efficiency, and its omnipresence are not just the result of shrewd marketing strategies, nor of rhetorical chicanery. Advertising is everywhere, speaking to everyone, *only* because the good that it manifests and portrays can exist everywhere, and is immediately recognizable to everyone—a chameleon-like substance that can take on the appearance and nature of everything around it.

As a total moral project, advertising is just the symptom and the consequence of a moral revolution, more than an economic one—a revolution whose import we have yet to gauge. Modernity, it has been said,[23] was born of and built upon the triumph of ordinary life—those parts of life tied to the humblest dimensions of work, to the manufacture of everyday objects, to family and sexuality—overturning every hierarchy that had placed contemplative or political activities at the apex of the moral ladder. And this same daily life was, for centuries, the favorite subject of the novel and of literature.[24] Advertising discourse simply radicalizes this same logic, enacting a small but decisive shift: if the good is everywhere, if it can accompany us in every situation and in all biographic, geographic, social, or cultural conditions, that's because its nature is not purely human. The good now corresponds to the very shape of things—their color, their scent, their weight, all those secondary qualities that philosophy has long denied any right of citizenship, become the shape in which value exists—the presence of the good on earth. From this perspective, advertising is an immense collective organ that allows us to fix our attention upon this form of the good, an eye that allows us to see the good where it's never before been possible to see it. This is not some kind of magical process that changes things into symbols or fetishes. Advertising is an organ of judgment vis-à-vis a good commensurate with the infinite forms that matter can assume. The realism of advertising is nothing other than the moral response to the transformation of the moral structure of the universe: we live in a world where the good coincides with the material, with things themselves. Only because of this can advertising moralize things, inscribing our relationship with things within a moral sphere, thereby transforming our relationship to the material—which had mostly been conceived of as an adiaphoron—into something in which our perfection is at stake. It is in things that we find moral strength. It is things—their shape, their appearance, their design— that allow us to take part in what for centuries we have called the good.

The paradox of the commodity is both deeper and stranger than what critical philosophy seems to hold. To understand this it's necessary, at least for a moment, to try to take seriously how advertising never tires of repeating itself. Being fulfilled in our relationships to commodities is not so much (or not only) a physical or economic need, but a moral necessity, or rather the moral necessity par excellence: the need for happiness. Just as cities formerly defined their models of perfection, identified the ultimate source of virtue, and tried to imagine an absolute form of happiness through their relations to gods, heroes, and history, so in the same way do our cities try to formulate and resolve ethical quandaries through their relationship to commodities. The system of needs that commodities embody is not only a means of managing the relationship between men and things. It is also—

and especially—the way to create a moral order that is no longer embodied in actions and gestures, no longer has intersubjectivity as its chosen site, and is no longer crystalized in the contemplation of that which exists beyond the world and things.

The new morality that advertising claims to express and prophesize is not generated in the gestures of an individual relating to herself or to God, but in the diffuse and quotidian relation by which she links herself to the universe of things that she herself produces, exchanges, consumes, and uses. Perhaps it is this that seems hard to accept: if one lends credence to what the city's stones proclaim every day, man needs things—disparate and everyday objects—to produce a moral order. It's as if through advertising the city were confessing that it cannot help but live in things and through things, for reasons that are moral rather than economic or commercial—as if, in advertising, humans revealed their most disturbing side, revealing themselves as organisms that are ethically inseparable from the very things they produce, exchange, and desire. In the advertising imaginary, man is a moral cyborg, whose existence attains ethical perfection only via the universe of things. The necessary alienation that commodities cause and express is moral rather than economic or social; we need our own products not so much—or not only—to survive biologically or to improve the physical conditions of our existence, but to live morally.

At first blush, it's not easy to see why a moral order should need things, products, or objects of daily use. How, indeed, could a thing make our nature more morally perfect? In what way can an object be the source and form of a happy life, the source and end of an ethos or of a perfect way of life? These doubts seem to raise problems of two different orders. On the one hand, in fact, our cities' obsession with commodities, their weight in the space and time of our lives, seems to cast doubt on the clearest tenets of moral knowledge that have been handed down to us through the centuries. If it is things that give us perfection and happiness, what is the stuff of our moral existence? Are our ways of life really only skin-deep? And is it really just our intentions, feelings, or aspirations that determine the moral quality of gestures and actions, inclinations and events, in our lives? Making commodities the most recent name of the good means recognizing that the limits of our morality align neither with the contours of our anatomy nor with the spiritual iridescence of our intentional acts. If it is things that render us morally perfect, art and craft are suddenly forms of ethical knowledge: art and craft will have to define the categories of this new moral order. Conversely, if in things we find not only material utility and sustenance for biological life, but also the supreme moral good, it will no longer be possible to see things as simple instruments or screens upon which we project a significance born elsewhere—a significance deformed or mutated by the laboratory of things. In advertising, the status of the object rises to an unprecedented dignity that must be interrogated: a form of the good's existence that manifests neither as action, nor as contemplation, nor still as relation to one's self. Things no longer have a simple economic or biological utility—they are no longer defined by exchange value or possible use; they are moral sources that allow anyone who comes into contact with them to participate in some way in a good that can only be experienced through them.

A good that can only exist as a produced and exchanged object makes practical inquiry and moral inquiry coincide. On the one hand, asking ourselves how we become perfect will mean asking ourselves what we do with things, and what things do in the world we live in. On the other hand, interrogating mechanical production and its meaning in contemporary life will mean interrogating the motives that moved contemporary society to construct a moral order (which it needs to become happy and to see itself as happy) in a form other than contemplation, one's relationship to oneself, or a well-tempered and orderly sociability. Why have we needed this extension of moral life? Why did we have to stretch moral life into a sphere from which it was traditionally excluded?

In intensifying commodities' production, exchange, consumption, and advertising, a new form of objectified morality was created, one that changes the status of the existence of things—and in particular of human life. Commodities in effect constitute a new objectified morality that causes the good to take on shapes that the body, praxis, and social life are unable to produce. They extend moral life into spheres impenetrable by pure sociability. From this perspective, a commodity, much more than a simple consumer good, is an organ that allows us to try out this new type of good. To understand this, one need only think about the peculiar nature of artifacts: each one, far from representing a simple extension of a bodily organ or a simple amplification of man's natural, organic activities, in fact allows us to carry out otherwise-impossible tasks and to radically transform the space and time of human existence.[25] It is thanks to mechanical production that man lives in the world and is not locked in the world.[26] An airplane or a telephone radically amplifies the spatial and temporal limits of man's universe—it alters not just man's life, but the very world in which that life unfolds, erasing from it any and all types of essence. By means of mechanical production, the human world swells with possibilities, overcoming its objective quality and thus growing more indeterminate. Commodities enact an analogous function in the sphere of morality: they open up for man a moral dimension that doesn't, by nature, belong to him; they take the moral world beyond its ordinary quality and render it more expansive, more indeterminate, more disturbing. Through commodities, moral life extends itself past the limits of praxis, contemplation, and sociability, absorbing as its sources all the objects we can possibly encounter. Morality loses its purely human nature, becoming infinitely malleable.

Charles Larmore has identified the basic characteristics of the good in modernity as heterogeneity and contingency. Freed from religion, the modern good is a plural and heterogeneous mass that exists as a profusion of "different moral principles that urge independent claims upon us . . . and so can draw us in irreconcilable ways."[27] From this perspective, evil is not the absence of the good, but rather its excess: there is evil—whose real name, put more simply, is complexity—only because there are too many goods that we cannot reconcile into a singularity—only because "the ultimate sources of moral value are not one, but many."[28] And if the good has lost its singularity, it has also lost any link to essence—so much so that the good is no longer directly inferable from the essence of the object that it refers to. The most profound happiness is that which comes "as if from the outside," taking us by surprise.[29] "The happiness that life affords us is less often the good we can see reason to pursue than the unexpected good that befalls us when we are not expecting it,"[30] and thus, "that only luck can reveal to us."[31]

The system of commodities simply expands this movement, multiplying the moral sources of value until they amount to the totality of things—until it makes of everything, however ordinary, ephemeral, or short-lived, an incarnation of the good—until it makes good and material coincide. It's an extreme metaphysical stubbornness that endeavors to make the good coincide with the material and that struggles to extract the good, in all its forms, from the material. Capitalism has thus not brought about the disappearance or diminishment of morality, but rather its most radical and extreme expansion, up to the very limits of the extant and the real. Pens, shoes, and cars; houses, boats, and perfumes: the good is now everywhere.

4

TOTEM

The most barbarous or bizarre rituals and strangest myths translate
some human need, some aspect of life, whether individual or social.
—EMILE DURKHEIM, *THE ELEMENTARY FORMS
OF RELIGIOUS LIFE* (1912)

A curious and paradoxical fate weighs upon our relationship to things in
the West. Things are everywhere, and certainly not by chance: it is to
things, much more than to men or gods, that we have entrusted and still
daily entrust our history, our destiny, and our future. Things are what preserve a community's memory and spirit much more faithfully and lastingly
than individuals; we have to ask books and stones about dead civilizations
once their last surviving members have disappeared. Our own existences
are defined above all by the things that we use, imagine, and desire. And
yet a very old and inexplicable discomfort surprises us every time we try to
declare our love for things. The history of religion supplies the clearest
example of this. For centuries, it made of this a point of honor. In the West,
one could worship and venerate anything: unlikely anthropomorphic divinities who lived on mountain tops, aniconic gods who refused to have
their likenesses made, momentary divinities whose names alone survived
them, half-human liberators born by parthenogenesis who could come back to
life after death, incorporeal angels and demons who nonetheless needed
wings, animae mundi along with saints, prophets, and emperors. Anything
could become a cult object—anything, that is, except a thing, regardless of
whether it was man-made or found in nature. It was only ever "others"—the
barbarians among ancient peoples, the savages among foreigners—who

adhered to the cult of things. The testimonies of travelers and scholars here seemed to converge: elsewhere people worshiped "the first material object that each nation or individual was inclined to choose and to make consecrated in ceremonies performed by its priests; this could be a tree, a mountain, the sea, a piece of wood, a petrified lion's tail, a shell, salt, a fish, a plant, a flower, a certain species of animal, such as cow, goat, elephant, sheep—in sum, any such thing that one can imagine."[1] Elsewhere things "are just so many Gods, sacred things, and talismans," and people "worship them assiduously and respectfully, address their wishes to them, offer them sacrifices, display them in processions if possible, or carry them around with great signs of veneration and consult them on all important occasions, generally regarding them as the guardians of men, and as powerful protection against all kinds of accidents."[2]

It was Charles de Brosses, in a famous study published in Geneva in 1760, who gave the name of *fetishism* to this uninhibited and forbidden love for things. By talking of fetishism rather than idolatry—and thus turning what used to be condemned as idolatry into a "habit of thought" proper to a variety of populations, de Brosses founded the anthropology of religion[3] and made comparativism possible.[4] And the notion of fetishism, "the problematic idea that became a kind of cornerstone for the social sciences of the nineteenth century,"[5] continued to trouble every study of man and his psychic and social life, from psychoanalysis to philosophy, and from anthropology to economics.[6]

It's hard to understand what the source of this unease may be. It's easier to enumerate its symptoms and the forms it takes. It was probably Augustine who provided the most ambiguous and influential version of this. In the context of a phenomenology of our relationship to things, Augustine identifies two possible relationships to the objects that surround us: *loving enjoyment* [*frui*] and instrumental use. "There are some things, then, which are to be enjoyed," he writes, "others which are to be used. . . . Those things which are objects of enjoyment make us happy. Those things which are objects of use assist, and (so to speak) support us in our efforts after happiness, so that we can attain the things that make us happy and rest in them."[7] Our relationship to things is, in any case, some kind of love. The difference between enjoyment and use lies only in the ardor and the end of this love: if enjoying a thing means "to rest with satisfaction in it for its own sake,"[8] in use, the thing is subordinate to what one really loves. And yet, in the same passage where he provides a name for the relationship to things that is not simple instrumental use, Augustine seems to want to distance himself from that relationship. Recalling that every Christian is on earth as though he were traveling in a foreign land, Augustine speaks of the enjoyment of things as an illicit use, an abuse [*usus inlicitus, abusus*]. "The true objects of enjoyment, then," he writes, "are the Father and the Son and the Holy Spirit, who are at the same time the Trinity, one Being, supreme above all, and common to all who enjoy Him, if He is an object, and not rather the cause of all objects, or indeed even if He is the cause of all."[9] Love for things is only possible as a form of sublimation. One might think—as Freudian and Lacanian psychoanalysis essentially has—that Augustine is simply describing a mechanism inherent in the very nature of desire, which cannot stop at an object: within or behind every beloved object there must always be another one hiding, albeit one of paradoxical status.[10] But it's hard to explain the emergence of a taboo with a diagnosis of impossibility; if love for a thing were really impossible or were only accessible via an intermediary object (however partial or metonymic), then there would be no reason to prohibit it.

In Augustine's words, we can surely hear the echo of the Judeo-Christian taboo against idolatry. But it would be naïve to ascribe to our uneasy rejection of the love of things a purely "religious" genealogy. In reality, we are not dealing with a taboo fully encompassed by religion, but rather with a motive that pervades all spheres of moral reflection, from philosophical ethics to literature and the social sciences—a motive that also emerges in an infinite variety of minor, vernacular forms of morality or codes of etiquette, which are adopted in social spaces circumscribed by time or place (i.e., courts, monasteries, families). It's as if, in reflecting upon its relationship to things, the West has obsessively tried to reformulate the ancient Platonic maxim that holds that the good is always *epekeina tês ousias* [*Republic*, VI, 509b9]—beyond being and beyond all entities, and thus beyond all things.

And it's in our relationship to commodities that the secular discomfort we experience every time we talk about, think of, or use things is most forcefully expressed. There is nothing coincidental about this bad faith: "commodity" is the category we use today to try to conceive of the value of things, to express the fact that the good is in things. Thinking about commodities means thinking about the good *in* things, the good *of* things—and, vice versa, trying to think about the good *as* a thing. And the reflections that have accompanied this explosion of love, attention, and thought given to things only seem to extend this ancient and sickening prohibition.

It was Marx who first spoke of fetishism in relation to commodities, and since then there have been infinite variations on the theme.[11] De Brosses had used the term *fetish* to designate a kind of symbolic excess typical of things that had become cult objects or objects of worship. Fetish, he wrote, is a "term coined by our merchants in Senegal based on the Portuguese word *fetisso*, meaning a thing that is magical, enchanted, or capable of producing oracles; from the Latin root *Fatum, Fanum, Fari*."[12] The extraordinary value attributed to things is linked to their ability to speak—to a symbolic value that exceeds their material nature. For Marx, too, the fetishistic nature of things corresponds to a symbolic excess. Insofar as they are fetishes, commodities store and crystalize not simply use value, but a reflection of the social relations that made their production possible, and that is reflected in their *exchange value*. In becoming commodities, things begin to speak, to mean something more and something other than their own nature as useful objects or instruments. "The table continues to be wood, an ordinary, sensuous thing. But as soon as it emerges as a commodity, it changes into a thing which transcends sensuousness. It not only stands with its feet on the ground, but, in relation to all other commodities, it stands on its head, and evolves out of its wooden brain grotesque ideas, far more wonderful than if it were to begin dancing of its own free will."[13] Insofar as they are fetishes, commodities can speak, but they can't speak about themselves: they become impotent mirrors of the society that produced them, and the images they reflect obscure their own true appearance.

In an infinite variety of ways, this diagnosis has marked most of our thinking about our relationship to commodities, radicalizing its impact. Thus, to the idea that, for a thing, being a commodity means possessing a symbolic value in excess of its nature and basic utility, it has been rightfully objected that it is above all in its use value that a commodity becomes a symbol. "Use value is not less symbolic or less arbitrary than commodity value. Utility is not a quality of the object but a significance of the objective qualities."[14] In other words, "what stamps trousers as masculine and skirts as feminine has no necessary connection with their physical properties . . . it is by their correlations in a symbolic system that pants are produced for men and skirts for women rather than by the nature of the object per se or its capacity to satisfy a material need."[15] It is only this symbolic value that renders things susceptible to exchange.[16] "No object, no thing, has being or movement in human society, except by the significance men can give to it."[17] Precisely because of this, "objects are the carriers of indexed social significations, of a social and cultural hierarchy—and this in the very least of their details: form, material, colors, durability, arrangement in space—in short, it is certain that they constitute a code."[18] Things qua commodities are reduced to mere human "concepts" that exist outside the mind, "like a man speaking to a man through the medium of things."[19] But these words do not help one to understand the world: the language of things is only the narcissistic reflection of a community that projects its own face onto things, and uses them to speak only of itself. Using these codes will never mean seeing the world—only the society that produced them.[20] Like the totems of ancient times,[21] the mass of commodities is supposedly just a system of classification via intermediary objects. And in producing and exchanging things, a society supposedly just reproduces itself symbolically—reproduces its own internal articulation, and its own cleavages.

In the classic analysis, then, goods transform into "distinctive signs," symbols, or sacraments through which a society performatively reproduces cleavages that cannot help but be present in things. This diagnosis, which has even enabled the discovery of a possible way of relating to things (what Veblen called "conspicuous consumption"[22]), seems nonetheless to be informed by the same discomfort that has weighed for centuries upon Western morality. The Augustinian prohibition against loving things in and of themselves is in fact transformed in this kind of analysis into an ontological impossibility: the immediate enjoyment of things *for what they are* is no longer simply forbidden, it is declared socially impossible. There is no possible immediate access to the world of things: if the nature and utility of things is immediately absorbed into their symbolic character—into their being social symbols— the love of things is quite simply the narcissism of a society incapable of doing anything but talking about itself, with its every gesture.

No attempt at repression is really effective. The completely theoretical prohibition on enjoying and loving things the way one loves a god, man, or hero has always been accompanied in concrete reality by practices: an infinite series of transgressions, sanctioned or legitimated thanks to slight *détournements* (re-routings). Precisely because it was condemned, repressed, or forbidden, a love for things (an uninhibited love) always returned, turning up in the most unusual forms.[23] It is not commodities that enable a different relationship to things, one that sees them as receptacles of a good generally thought to reside elsewhere. In contemporary society, art sanctions a relation to material objects and artifacts that is perfectly commensurate with this worship. In relating to works of art, that *ordo amoris* (order of love) demanding that we separate and oppose love for things from love for persons seems entirely dismantled. Alfred Gell, in a remarkable book dedicated to developing an anthropology of art, made this point most forcibly, showing how in the entire sphere of relations to objects that we call "art," the relationship to things is perfectly equivalent to that which one has with persons. Considering objects to be artistic means attributing agency to them—in other words, that same capacity to initiate "causal sequences of a particular type, that is, events," which we usually attribute to human subjects—and seeing them as "'caused' by themselves, by their intentions, not by the physical laws of the cosmos."[24] To the eye of an ethnographer, this manifests not as a pure symbolic system, but above all as a "system of action" made of objects "that mediate social intentionality" and that exist socially like *just so many scattered persons*.[25] "The anthropology of art," in short, "is the theory of art which 'considers art objects as persons,'" just as, according to Mauss, "gifts" could be considered as persons or as their extensions.[26] Attributing intentions and consciousness to things is a much more common behavior than we generally assume (one need only think, for example, about the relationship children have with their dolls, or many adults have with their cars). Art legitimates, "crystallizes," and institutionalizes a way of relating to things that doesn't have the same degree of longevity and legitimacy elsewhere.[27] From the anthropological point of view, art is thus a specific case of the relation to objects that in other contexts is called animism or idolatry. Considering an object as a person, for all that, does not mean attributing biological life to it: "'agency' is not defined in terms of 'basic' biological attributes (such as inanimate thing vs. biological person), but is relational . . . what matters is where it stands in a network of social relations";[28] and in order for an object to be recognized as a person—

that is, as a social agent—it is not at all necessary for it to possess life in a biological sense. Precisely because, as part of a sphere of artistic objects, a thing appears to us "like a person," it is possible to direct toward it the love, attention, and care that it is permissible to give to people. Worship of an artwork directly corresponds to the worship of an artist and his or her spirit. From this point of view, in the system of objects, contemporary art constitutes a kind of return of the repressed: forbidden, censured commodity fetishism here becomes a form of cultural and moral virtuosity.

But it is not only in the perfect interchangeability of love for things and love for persons that the artistic object represents the return of the fetishistic repressed. In the artistic object, the tragic dialectic between value and utility, or between good and nature, that seemed to leave its stamp upon the commodity suddenly appears to have vanished. The common thinking is that, insofar as it is a commodity, everything seems to be cleft by an internal fracture: on the one hand, there's its nature or its possible use, and on the other hand, a totally arbitrary social value, not inferable from the first. Production not only alienates labor power from the worker, making it reside outside of him; it also alienates it from nature, from the world of things[29]—it separates labor power from the world in which things show themselves for what they are. It's as if, in order to conceive of a thing as a social good, it were necessary to stop thinking about its nature and utility—or, vice versa, as if, in thinking about the nature of things, it were impossible to think of them as social goods. In a commodity, the good is in things, but it is not identical to their nature, understood as use value. From this point of view, Marxist thought seems to repeat Platonic *logion*: thinking about the good of things means thinking about something that exceeds their nature; and conversely, thinking about the nature of things means not thinking about their value. In the work of art, on the other hand, nature and value, good and utility, seem to correspond, and not through the equilibrium that comes from being mutually exclusive.

Art is not the only sphere where things can appear as subjects: technology proliferates hybrids, and in fact distinguishes itself ever more markedly as the sphere in which the subjectivity of things is knowingly assumed as a productive end and an obvious fact.[30] But mechanically produced objects capable of acting and looking "like a person" elicit a cultural diffidence that is foreign to the realm of art. If in art the subjectivity of things is the echo or reflection of the human subjectivity that produced it, technology and manufacturing struggle to show how things and materials possess a proper, immanent spiritual subjectivity that is not the result of a projection.

The emergence of industrial art—what we generally call design—is quite simply the form in which art, manufacturing, and commerce seem to reach an utterly novel resolution: the love for things that art made permissible is extended to nearly all objects of daily use;[31] life tends to mix itself up with art, and art with the spheres of production and commerce.[32] Just as design is "the planning . . . of everything that creates the environment in which man lives today," so advertising is the total moralization of the human world.[33]

Art, manufacturing, and commerce are three spheres in which man, in various forms and with different degrees of license and intensity, experiences his love for things. Like in any true love, free will and necessity are inextricably intertwined here. We can't help but love the objects that surround us, adoring them, investing time, intellectual energy, and care in them—we have no other choice. We are subjects not simply in front of things, or before them, but always through them, by means of them. All things are mediums because it is always by means of something, within the horizon created by our relation to things, that we are and that we become someone. It's not that we attribute to things a subjectivity that rightfully lies with us, and neither do things exist objectively. People do not exist outside of the relation to things. We are people, we become people, only in the midst of things: in a house, on the street, on a chair, with a pair of shoes. Complete nudity, the possibility of not having things, of not being in the midst of them, is just a myth for theologians. It's what, to emphasize its alienating and negative effects, has been called reification. But by dint of concentrating on the risks, excesses, and possible evils, we forget that there's a splendor and a euphoria in coinciding with things and their form, which each of us feels in the act of creation. The painter aspires to reify his gaze on the canvas; the craftsman or designer struggles to capture the human spirit in an object; and every novel is a process of reification. "It matters little whether it does good or ill," wrote Flaubert in a letter, "writing is a marvelous thing: not being yourself anymore, traveling all around the creation that one is talking about. Today, for example, as man and woman, together, lover and beloved, simultaneously, I rode on horseback through a forest, on an autumn afternoon under yellow leaves. I was the horse, the leaves, the wind, the words that they said, and the reddening sun that made their eyes half-close under the weight of love."[34] Every creative act is a reification—a successful reification. In every creative act, we coincide for a moment with the world of things: there's a positively moral quality in every *act of reification*.

From a certain perspective, the modern debate about reification seems to retrace and repeat the themes of the eighteenth-century "querelle du luxe" (the luxury controversy).[35] Commodities, exactly like luxury, are supposed to owe "their birth to our vices" (because they are supposed to be the fruit of a desire to earn and accumulate), and theoretically they generate a "dissolution of morals," which "brings with it in its turn the corruption of taste."[36] Rousseau's words could perfectly summarize various contemporary claims.[37] To these arguments one might reply with Voltaire's verses (the ones that provoked Rousseau's response) that "tout sert au luxe, aux plaisirs de ce monde" (everything serves luxury, serves worldly pleasures), and "le superflu, chose très nécessaire, / a réuni l'un et l'autre hémisphère" (the superfluous, a very necessary thing, / has united both hemispheres)—or argue that "the more men refine upon pleasure, the less will they indulge in excesses of any kind."[38] The relationship to things and to the good they incarnate is an instrument of spiritual elevation and psychic sublimation.

It would be fruitless to continue to gather arguments for one side or the other. Not only is the debate ancient,[39] but these two positions also, now as in the past, seem to take the same principle as their starting point. One and the same conviction unites the city walls' songs of praise for the things we use, the savant discourse that modern liberalism has produced about the civilizing power of luxury, and the ancient and modern condemnation of commodities' or luxury's capacity to corrupt, to make societies and tastes barbaric again. In all these cases, things are defined morally, as ethical forces even prior to being material realities: for better or for worse, things—commodities—are sources of happiness or perfection, causes of perdition or evil—but they are never morally indifferent.

The entry for *luxe* in the *Encyclopédie* explained that the use "of wealth and industry to obtain a pleasant way of life" has as its primary cause "our lack of satisfaction with our situation, our yearning to be better off, that is, and must be, in all men."[40] What's revealed in the propensity toward wealth—that upon which we found the system of production, circulation, and accumulation of things that we call economy—is a desire to be better, to go beyond our own situation.[41] Before or beneath interest or the desire for social distinction is a force moral in nature, which draws us to things or pushes us away from them—which, in short, determines our relationship with the world, for better or for worse. Even the choice of poverty paradoxically invests the universe of things with a moral value in addition to its economic one, and transforms the world of objects—that is, nearly all material things—into a sort of extra-anatomical and nonhuman ethical life. From this point of view, advertising and social philosophy seem indistinguishable.

The status, forms, and causes of this moral force coincident with things are hard to understand; the morality of things seems to be taken for granted by philosophy, economics, and common sense, but is only rarely interrogated as such. Before we decide in what sense the things that we call commodities (that is, nearly all the objects that surround us, that we desire and use) exert a moral influence upon us—before glorifying or condemning them, consenting to them or cursing them—it is possible and necessary to try to understand how a thing—an inanimate substance—can become a moral phenomenon, giving life to an ethos beyond our bodies.

5

THE WORLD OF THINGS

World—be, and be good;
behave nicely,
see to it that, try to, aim at, tell me all.

—ANDREA ZANZOTTO, "TO THE WORLD"

"The life of money-making is a constrained kind of life, and clearly wealth is not the Good we are in search of, for it is only good as being useful, a means to something else."[1] For centuries, ethics has sought and found new formulations of this Aristotelian sentence: the good must exist outside of or beyond things, because things are means, instruments, and not ends of human existence. Economics was born the moment we attempted to overturn this judgment, and to recognize, in the words of Montchrestien, that "the happiness of men ... principally consists in richness and richness comes from work."[2] Going from condemning wealth to framing it as the ultimate end of human existence demands more than just logic and speculation: if, as Montchrestien himself admitted, wealth consists in work—is produced through work—then it was only a long series of social transformations (transformations enabling work to be seized upon as the means by which every individual reaches her own perfection) that socially synthesized the correspondence between the good and things.[3]

From a certain point of view, modern thought (not just the branch of economics) is simply an enormous effort to conceive of and synthesize the articulation between good and material in the guise of wealth. The long, elaborate history of this effort has been written many times, and the evidence of a world entirely constructed by production and circulation is overlaid by a multitude of perceptions and stories that are difficult to re-compose as one. Advertising, at its heart, is simply one of these infinite discourses—the wildest and most popular one. It would be difficult, there-fore, to make it into a mere epiphenomenon or expression of economic thought, as if it were a kind of translation for the vast ignorant masses of what economists try to understand in a more refined way, or a malicious mise-en-scène of market actors' economic practices. Advertising is not comparable to iconographic communications aimed at secular society—it is not an image, as Saint Gregory the Great famously put it,[4] that allows even the illiterate to see and understand.

What makes impossible nearly any direct conflation of advertising and economics is advertising's irrepressible rhetorical-epistemological, socio-logical, and even material independence compared to the vast majority of disciplines whose object is the economic life of nations and cities (i.e., eco-nomics, sociology, law). Produced by subjects (ad writers) whose professions, skills, and training are different from those of the people producing and vulgarizing economics and the social sciences, advertising turns out to be stylistically and epistemologically much closer to the Renaissance literature of emblems and personal devices than to practically any scholarly work,[5] and it tends to appear in different forms and different physical and social con-texts than other discourses about commodities, value, and money do.

Nor is this a case of an ex post interpretation of economic phenomena, or of a detached description of them. Advertising seems altogether to be a more deeply seated discourse, but also a more hyperbolic, obsessive, man-nered one. It's deeper than the very facts of economic life, because it's re-puted to anticipate and virtually provoke consumer actions—that is, actions by a segment of the subjects moving in the marketplace. It seeks not to de-scribe but to cause the phenomenon it speaks of,[6] and precisely for this reason, it tends to transform it, to such a degree that it is not fully expressed in the act that it provokes, like the images and feelings that live in the mind of someone possessed by an infatuation. It is as if, through advertising, it were possible to access a more deeply buried level than what economics, or even consumer sociology, examines: in advertising discourse, it's the dreamed-of dynamics of consumption, and not its actual practice, that gets expressed.

In this sense, advertising can't provide the same description of economic life, its actors' motives, and its objects as one finds in the economic sciences. It doesn't use the same concepts or the same language as sociology or economics because the world of which it speaks is radically different. In advertising discourse, the focus is no longer on money, work, trade, or even the desire to accumulate profits or capital. The focus is on things and their capacity to morally transform human life. And the same commodity can appear to have a completely different nature and different attributes when it appears in the medium of any advertising poster than when it shows up in a work of economics or sociology. It's not only more colorful, more "real," more alive. Its very value is different, the way in which it is a good. In the medium of advertising, a commodity is only accidentally defined by a price or an exchange value: an ad has quite rightly to demonstrate that the objective value of a commodity is infinitely superior to its price—that it's a good of a wholly different nature than that of mere money. Very often, the commodity also defines itself in spite of its utility. This is not only or not so much because we are largely dealing here with objects that don't fill any real need (the reality of needs is much less clear-cut than we normally think)[7]— but rather because, in a classic inversion, in an advertising message the object is no longer an instrument by which human needs are fulfilled, but on the contrary, the individual or the consumer is the means through which the aesthetic, moral, and social existence of the advertised object can be fulfilled.[8] In advertising, in short, everything is a good on the basis of mechanisms different from those studied by economics; everything acquires a moral value distinct from its express exchange and use values.[9]

Analyzing this discourse, recognizing the truth that it formulates without tracing it back either to economic theory or to social dynamics of a merely strategic interest, means recognizing that the economic order proper to capitalism is much less monolithic and uniform than either its theorists or its adversaries would like to believe. The very existence of advertising, the real or imagined necessity of its presence as part of the normal course of economic life, might seem to show ipso facto that what we generally define as political economy emerges thanks to the coexistence of completely incompatible branches of knowledge and develops simultaneously in multiple spheres of existence, both from a moral and from a metaphysical point of view. The life of commodities is not exhausted by the processes of production, distribution, exchange, and consumption: commodities today also live in an ulterior space, independent from the real one even if related to it—that of advertising, where they take on specific features. This *ontological* multiplicity corresponds to a moral multiplicity. Things acquire value—

they are good—not simply thanks to production and exchange; there is a process of moralization in things that remains autonomous, as independent from work as it is from money, which remains to be examined.

We can examine how things come into the world and ask the work that generates them to reveal the secret of their nature. We need only "trace some of the ordinary provisions of life, through their several progresses, before they come to our use" to discover how things "receive . . . their value from human industry."[10] From Locke onward, this has been the anthropological premise of modernity: "labour makes the far greatest part of the value of things we enjoy in this world."[11] Things can be the site of existence of the good—can have value—because they have been produced, because labor "added something to them more than nature, the common mother of all, had done."[12] It was this same premise that came to comprise the basis of Adam Smith's theory of value,[13] and later Marx's as well—a theory that made commodities into the set of things that can accumulate, crystalize, and coagulate the social material called labor. Commodities are by these lights things understood as "coagulated labor time,"[14] and with that labor time comes the social divisions labor carries. Such a definition makes a commodity into an essence rather than a state: things are commodities as a function of how they are constituted. But there are quite a few things that do not come into the world as commodities, and instead become them: things that gain value, or become "goods," not as a function of the time needed to produce them that has accumulated in them. To the point of view of classic modernity (that represented by Locke, Smith, and Marx, among others), it has been rightly objected (most incisively by Georg Simmel) that the metaphysical space that enables things to acquire value—to become goods—is not labor but rather exchange. It's not because things have value that exchange comes about; on the contrary, exchange or its possibility is the source of a thing's value.[15]

We can thus observe the life history of things, and trace the path that, step by step, exchange by exchange, allows them to achieve their end, to transform into use. It is as a function of the possibility of becoming an exchange object ("a sociological phenomenon sui generis, an original form and function of social life")[16] that anthropology has preferred to define commodities.[17] From this point of view, indeed, everything can become a "commodity,"[18] even bartered objects; here, the title of "commodity" no longer designates a substance, or gathers a class of things separated by their nature from other things by virtue of having accumulated in themselves the paradigmatic social substance. "Commodity" from this perspective just describes a state, a particular situation in which things can find themselves. Things then ought to contain the potential to become a commodity. The state of being a commodity is in this view a limited phase in the social life of things, a situation or phase defined as a function of exchange,[19] and thus culturally regulated even before it is economically regulated—indeed, what allows something to become an object of exchange or not are often cultural criteria rather than economic ones.[20] From this perspective, a thing can become or cease to be a commodity through processes (of commodification or decommodification) that can never describe its entire biography.

But understanding things' capacity to crystallize value, to make the good exist in material form—that is, understanding their existence qua commodities—as a state that only temporarily affects things does not explain why a commodity continues to exert its power (and to have social value) after it has passed through an exchange. Even after we've acquired them, we continue to use things and to acknowledge that they have value in excess of their basic utility. The value that commodities have—the good that they succeed at crystalizing and that transforms them into something more than simple instruments—is not a mere social or cultural whim, for the same reasons that it can't be reduced to a pure economic accident. If we don't stop investing time, energy, and imagination in producing, exchanging, and dreaming of things and commodities, that's because the good that they make present does not disappear immediately after their acquisition. The good of things is not a patina that society or culture can apply to or strip away from the material world at will—it is an originating force that one can exploit, but that cannot be conjured up out of thin air. In relating to things, we don't just relate to their possible use, because every commodity distills meanings and existences that utility cannot account for. Using a car means much more than being able to travel quickly. But in relating to us, each object does not simply reflect back to us a mirror image of the social properties of the labor that produced it. The shapes, colors, novelty, charm, and interest of the things that we use, acquire, or desire are neither simple symbols of social divisions nor mere conventions—they are the expression of a state of being that has nothing human about it. This is evinced by the fact that our relationship to things engages not just our social selves, but also our senses, our reason, our emotions—the entirety of a person. If the commodity is a total anthropological fact, it is because a person's whole existence in the world, not just her social being, is distilled and reified in her relation to things. In using and consuming things, each of us constructs our world and crystalizes the collection of cultural categories that define our being in the world:[21] "consumption is the very arena where culture is fought over and locked into shape."[22] Conversely, having a relationship to things—producing, acquiring, dreaming of, thinking about, or exchanging commodities—means changing the shape of the natural world we live in and belong to. This is why our relationship to commodities is always the crystallization of a kind of mobile cosmology.[23] The good that stands before us in every commodity is a social and an individual force—both cultural and natural.

A society never constitutes itself through itself: it has to objectify itself in something else. Civilizations have always needed to be incarnated and actualized in something they produce; whether via institutions, religions, myths, or cults, a population always constitutes, conceives of, and actualizes itself in something other than itself. This other, which is both instrument and site of a civilization's moral and spiritual fulfillment (what a certain tradition has called objective spirit),[24] is now particularly constituted by the mass of commodities and by their exchange—that is, by commerce. If our society recognizes itself, feels its own pulse, and comes to understand itself only in commodities, then philosophy should start to study this sphere *iuxta propria principia*, without tracing it back to other expressions of human spiritual life, and without assuming that law, religion, or the arts are necessarily nobler.

The morality conveyed by advertising is entirely intra-worldly: it does not promise salvation from this world, but rather delineates how the things of the world make themselves into objectified happiness. A medieval church represented and displayed utopian, otherworldly geographies that one entered after death, with a new body. The modern city, on the other hand, proposes itself as the site of happiness: a paradise of things. If a city is humanity's magnum opus, the greatest thing we are capable of creating, then the contemporary city paints itself as a *happy* thing, insofar as it's the place that brings together all the things of this world, the seeds of happiness sown there—not a gathering of happy men, but the collection of those things that *are* happiness.

To conceive of the good as no longer "beyond being," but rather as perfectly commensurate with the things of this world, entails joining morality and cosmology. Of course, we are dealing here with a specific kind of world—this is not the world described by physics, but rather a collection of artifacts, of things that are manufactured, desired, distributed, consumed, and fantasized about publicly. The immutable order of the ancients' cosmos, with its *taxis* reflecting a superior form of intelligence, is now replaced by the mobile order of the market and of perpetual exchange, which is seen as the ultimate source of every form of happiness. If things in the ancient world aspired to a place in an immutable order that was the reflected existence of a superior good, now the being to which things aspire is exchange. The morality of things does not describe a psychology—it does not coincide with correct decisions: morality coincides with the order of good things, with the order of commodities—an order that is fundamentally mobile because it defines itself only through commerce and exchange.

In the end, the fact that nowadays the city—the political thing—can't stop talking to us about things, and only talks to us about people by means of commodities, should make us reflect more deeply upon another aspect of the present. In their very structure, in the marked tattooing of their very skin, contemporary cities show that a pure, absolute community of men without things has never existed and will never exist:[25] it is in things and through things that men can meet. Every city is a thing that only exists thanks to things. Cities are not and can never be purely human phenomena. They are a form of the world, a collection of things, not only of men. Europe itself is a political phenomenon born of an agreement (the Schengen Agreement) that sanctions equating the free movement of commodities and of men; we should then start to reflect upon the ways in which things and commodities themselves convey a form of sovereignty different from the state's.[26] The empires of the future may be defined by the mobile geography and sovereignty of commodities, which can create communities and identities without having to pass through the political establishment's traditional channels. There's a politics of things that still needs to be formulated and that represents the natural extension of the morality of things, which is incarnated in embryonic form by advertising.

We have always thought too little about the role that things play in the establishment of shared political and moral space. Plutarch tells us that at the moment of Rome's foundation, Romulus, in observance of an ancient Etruscan ritual, threw the first fruits of all things into a pit that was then closed up forever. The pit, Plutarch continues, had the same name as the universe: *mundus*, or world.[27] Beyond the strictly religious significance of this ritual, which is also described by Ovid and Giovanni Lido, it is not insignificant that Rome is established by constructing a closed space that symbolically safeguards all things and, through them, is the equivalent of the world. Deep down, every city is inclined to mistake itself for the whole world, and it can only do this with things—or to be precise, only through commodities. This is not then a purely religious issue. The commodity has always constituted the paradigmatic site of this union of city and cosmos. It is commodities, much more than people, that have always borne witness to the fact that the city is part of a bigger world; it is commodities that transport foreign elements, customs, ideas, and habits to a city.[28] It's a pious illusion to think that this phenomenon is tied to a "made in China" kind of modernity. Textiles, gems, pigments, as well as both rare foodstuffs and basic dietary staples (salt, sugar, oil)—it has *always* been the commodity that prevented cities from closing themselves off from the outside, the other. Today we generally prefer to use the sociological formula of "globalization" to express this lack of separation between city and cosmos, this inability to distinguish politics from ecology, or morality from economics, on a planetary scale. But the phenomenon is older and more profound than this. And it's always thanks to and through the commodity that this coupling has been consummated. The commodity is the first piece of evidence that our city is a whole world, not only in the sense that its limits go well beyond its walls, but also and especially in the sense that the city is something that cannot be reduced to the collection of men, subjects, or souls that live there: every city needs earth, elements, things. Thanks to the commodity, the city mistakes itself for the whole world, becoming inseparable or indistinguishable from it.

Even in its worldly character, in its capacity to make a world, the commodity attests to its status as the incarnation of good. The classical world recognized a strong link between the notion of the world and that of the good, a proximity suggested by the Greek term *kosmos*, which means beauty, ornament, elegance. As Pliny the Elder explains, "the Greeks have designated the world by a word that means 'ornament' [*kosmos*], and we have given it the name of *mundus*, because of its perfect finish and grace!"[29]

And it seems to have been Pythagoras who was "the first to call the world *kosmos* from the inherent order that reigns in it."[30] According to Alexander von Humboldt's ingenious formulation, *kosmos*—the world—is simply "the ornament of the ordered."[31] Speaking of the world always means speaking of beauty, of elegance, of the goodness of things, because, as one reads in Plato's *Gorgia*, "the specific *kosmos* innate in each thing is the good inherent in it."[32] For the ancients, the world is not the place where there's something rather than nothing, but where things are the presence of beauty and the good. Ancient cosmology managed to conceive of the panoply of things as a world—as a beautiful and elegant order—only by tracing them back to the mind of a demiurge, a creator, devoid of envy. As Plato writes, "God desired that, so far as possible, all things should be good and nothing evil; wherefore, when He took over all that was visible, seeing that it was not in a state of rest but in a state of discordant and disorderly motion, He brought it into order out of disorder (eis taxin auto egagen ek tes ataxias). . . . For Him who is most good it neither was nor is permissible to perform any action save what is most fair."[33] As paradoxical as it may sound, today it is advertising that takes upon itself this cosmogonic function. It is advertising that is "world-making"—it makes an inventory of things, just as they appear, christening them individually with first and last names (it does not speak to us of a generic "tomato soup," but rather of "Campbell's soup"). It describes them, organizes them, catalogues them, and tries to explicate the value of a thing, its good. Through advertising, even if in a clumsy and ever-incomplete way, our cities try to pass from disorder to order, and above all to grasp in every case the beauty that is in things: there is a splendor of reification that is the most radical form of being-in-the-world, with no way out. We must learn to pluck from advertising the truth that it harbors and continually proclaims. We never stop looking for and finding beauty in things and through things: a shoe, a shirt, a jacket, as well as a razor, makeup, or beauty creams. The good is in things, because *all* things are our ornament. They are, strictly speaking, our world.

6

TOWARD A MORAL HYPERREALISM

According to a widespread and generally agreed-upon idea, one of the distinctive features of late modernity is the exponential growth of reflexive kinds of knowledge. Contemporary societies are supposed not only to have produced and accumulated an unprecedented quantity of knowledge about themselves, their history, the happiness they seek, and the world around them, but also to have made accumulating and managing these very bodies of technical, sociological, moral, and scientific knowledge (along with reflections upon them) into the means by which they constitute and distinguish themselves.[1] It is not insignificant that in the public space parceled out by stone walls and their contemporary permutations (television sets, tablets, smartphones), the work of reflexivity focuses above all on things and merchandise. When the contemporary city starts to speak, it does so chiefly in order to transmit a certain form of understanding able to mirror and inform the behavior of social actors, that vernacular knowledge of things and commodities (and indirectly of the good life) conveyed by the monumental body of literature and iconography dedicated to commodities—advertising.

We can explain (and we have explained) this seeming anomaly in various ways. Sociologists and philosophers have correctly recognized in it the invasion of mercantile logic into the public sphere, the hegemony of the rules of economic life even over forms of morality, and the detachment of instrumental reason from the Lifeworld.[2] They have frequently pointed out, and quite rightly condemned, the excesses and illusions that advertising feeds and denounced the pathologies it creates. Without denying these arguments, I have wanted to focus here on the effects on our ethical sensibility and on the transformation of our moral universe that advertising to some extent causes and more significantly manifests. From the point of view of the historical *longue durée*, advertising essentially marks a substantive point of discontinuity, where public moral discourse no longer chiefly focuses on the relation between humans and the divine, nor on the relationship that man maintains with himself and his counterparts, but rather with things themselves, depicted as the primordial incarnation of the good. This is obviously not a radically new phenomenon: On the one hand, the moral philosophy that rippled out from the monastic rules of late antiquity and the middle ages gave great importance to the measure of one's relationship with things and with the material world (food, space, articles for daily use) in defining the monk's moral perfection. Franciscan thought, from this point of view, constitutes one pinnacle of this effort to bring the question of one's relationship to things (also in juridical terms) into the center of moral thought, such that it has been possible to see it as a testing ground for the economic categories of nascent capitalism.[3] On the other hand, the phenomenon of collecting, as Benjamin himself realized, seems to anticipate and prefigure many features of the moral obsession with things that characterizes contemporary "consumerism."[4]

But even such well-developed analogies are not able to erase an essential difference: even if, as in the Franciscan case, such concerns carried a good deal of weight, they were nonetheless always a matter of localized morality, presented as elite oppositions, addressed to small groups, and not cast as a public moral code imagined in universalist terms. The universalist ambitions of advertising's moral discourse (which by nature addresses any man or woman, even when it portrays one of its quintessential interlocutors) do not, of course, give it exclusive rights. It would be naïve and wrong to think that advertising comprised the *only* model of public ethics in our time; the moral discourses that articulate and guide contemporary life are infinite in number and diverse in form and content. But the material and discursive centrality of things and things qua commodities in the contemporary moral universe remains to my mind an undeniable piece of evidence, and it does not only turn up in advertising. When the new moralists invite us to consume intelligently and exhort us to renounce household appliances, exotic goods, or commodities that are particularly damaging to the environment or that are produced through forms of slavery, they position themselves within the very moral universe in which advertising is the paradigmatic form, and within which it is our relationship to things that determines our happiness and moral perfection. When new political movements place environmental or ecological concerns at the center of their agendas, they implicitly recognize that the key object of ethics and the site of the good's existence is the material world (or the world as material), and not humanity or divinity. This is the shift that struck me as interesting and unprecedented: a huge slice of reality, which for centuries was considered adiaphoron, becomes the preferred object of ethical thought. From this perspective, as we have seen, advertising, a certain form of social criticism, and a good number of contemporary moral philosophers seem to fit within the same framework and to bespeak the same moral sensibility. If I have concentrated on advertising rather than on analyzing all the manifestations of this new morality, this is not only because advertising is pervasive and somehow paradigmatic. Advertising is the primordial form of our moral code, one that has anticipated the forms, registers, and schemes of contemporary moral life; it has recognized the primacy of the iconic over the verbal; it has understood the psychagogic nature of moral experience and definitively surpassed the model of the philosophy of praxis, recognizing that happiness is not created by carrying out a *practical scheme*, but rather by elevating the individual to a superior level of existence—it has understood that there is no moral message without narrative or myth.

In short, it has been much better than other discourses or theories at capturing the moral sensibility of contemporary man. Admitting this does not mean championing the cause of unbridled consumerism, nor of giving one's blessing to the game of envy, selfishness, and base emotions that consumerism often encourages, but rather recognizing that the moral universe in which we live has a very different shape than the one traced by our history books. Trying to understand advertising as a particular form of morality different from those that preceded it, and freeing ourselves thus from the narrowly accusatory and to some extent paranoid gaze that political and social philosophy has directed at it is not a sign of nihilism, but rather that typically modern behavior often called political realism[5]—but with an important difference. This tradition, which in recent discussions has had its champions (one need look no further than Bourdieu, Foucault, or Girard), has always prided itself upon its unflinching willingness to look upon the totality of human experience, accepting and including humanity's despairs and miseries as an integral—indeed, the predominant—part of anthropology. It has often ended by understanding evil, power, and the struggle of every individual against everyone else as the moving principle of moral experience. In this book, on the contrary, I have tried to frame a pervasive, omnipresent phenomenon—one that is almost exclusively understood as the result of some indeterminate social ill—in positive moral terms, as a phenomenon sustained by a logic of production, a thirst, and a *jouissance* for a specific good. We might convey the sense of this kind of "moral hyperrealism" by reformulating an adage from Dostoevsky:[6] if God does not exist, then everything is good, and evil is just the effect of excess, or of a conflict between different goods. Or, to employ a slightly hackney formula from the history of philosophy, it is a question of moving from the Kant of the categorical imperative to the Hegel of the philosophy of right: pushing ourselves to maintain the anthropologist's point of view, we might conceive of the real order not as the result of a power that oppresses and alienates, but as the expression of a freedom (and thus of a morality) that is perhaps unpleasant, but is no less real than our own. Conceiving of humanity not in terms of what it is but in terms of what we would like it to be, Spinoza once wrote, means writing a satire, not an ethics.[7]

Recognizing that advertising has the status and the dignity of a public moral discourse—even if it's produced by and for the masses, with no plan, no global strategy, no edifying intention—doubtless entails desublimizing the moral universe to some extent. But one could argue that the public morality displayed on walls in other geographic and cultural contexts has almost never been marked by the sublime: celebrating battles that wiped out entire cultures in Roman bas-reliefs, worshiping imaginary deities in dead civilizations' temples, or glorifying the "client" in Christian frescoes is not per se more noble and sublime than inviting us to see the secret to happiness in a handbag. We must learn to look upon morality, and in particular upon its contemporary public form, with a gaze that is simultaneously more indulgent, less paranoid, and more rigorous than that of the teachers of the school of suspicion. In the end, this is one of the great lessons of the last century's anthropology: just like mythical creations, so too collective material practices—public myths and discourses through which humanity tries to make itself happy—are driven by a logic more closely resembling that of the *bricoleur* than the philosopher.

ACKNOWLEDGMENTS

The ideas in this book were presented in shorter form during a seminar at the Centre de Recherche sur les Arts et la Littérature in Paris (spring 2012), at a talk at the Festival of Philosophy in Modena, Italy (summer 2012), and during a course at the École des Hautes Études en Sciences Sociales in Paris (spring 2013). In addition to the sources cited above, I am deeply indebted to conversations and exchanges over the years with Raul Antelo, Esteban Buch, Flávia Cera, Michela Coccia, Iacopo Costa, Veronica Dari-Scolarod, Alessandro De Cesaris, Nicole Gabutti, Werner Hamacher, Julieta Hanono, Jakob Heller, Shinobu Iso, Bruno Karsenti, Marielle Macé, Elise Marrou, Antonella Martorano, Antonio Montefusco, Ron Naiweld, Alexandre Nodari, Anselm Oelze, Andrea Robiglio, Martin Rueff, Carlo Severi, Gianluigi Simonetti, Antonio Somaini, Massimo Vallerani, and Marta Zura Puntaroni.

Cinzia Arruzza, Daniele Balicco, Marcello Barison, Gianluca Briguglia, Elisa Brilli, Silvia Capodivacca, Matteo D'Alfonso, Emanuele Dattilo, Roberto Frega, Ilaria Gaspari, Francesca Lazzarin, Francesca Mambelli, Andrea Massi, Giuliano Milani, Giulia Oskian, Sylvain Piron, Francesca Sironi, Giovanni Sironi, Michele Spanò, and Caterina Zanfi also read, discussed, critiqued, and improved earlier versions of the book.

For a number of different reasons, Giorgio Agamben, Michelina Borsari, Lidia Breda, and Barbara Carnevali are at the origin of this book, and I would like to offer them a special thanks.

To Fabián Ludueña Romandini, I owe the experience of the good outside and next to things.

NOTES

PREFACE TO THE ENGLISH-LANGUAGE EDITION

1. Chiara Bottici, *Imaginal Politics: Images beyond the Imagination and beyond the Imaginary* (New York; Columbia University Press, 2014).

2. Paul Zanker, *Augustus und die Macht der Bilder* (Munich: Beck, 1987); David Freedberg, *The Power of Images: Studies in the History and Theory of Response* (Chicago: University of Chicago Press, 1989); W. J. T. Mitchell, *What Do Pictures Want?: The Lives and Loves of Images* (Chicago, University of Chicago Press, 2005).

3. Stephen Apkon, *The Age of the Image: Redefining Literacy in a World of Screens* (New York: Farrar, Straus and Giroux, 2013); Joan Fontcuberta, *La Cámara de Pandora: La fotografi despues de la fotografia* (Barcelona: Editorial Gustavo Gil, 2010). For a critical view, see Frederic Jameson, "Transformations of the Image in Postmodernity," in *The Cultural Turn: Selected Writings on the Postmodern, 1983–1998* (Verso: London and New York, 1998), 93–135; Stuart Ewen, *All Consuming Images: The Politics of Style in Contemporary Culture* (New York: Basic Books, 1988); and Daniel J. Boorstin, *The Image: A Guide to Pseudo-events in America* (New York: Athenaeum 1962).

4. Cf. Barbara Maria Stafford, *Artful Science: Enlightenment, Entertainment and the Eclipse of Visual Education* (Cambridge, MA, and London: MIT Press, 1994).

5. On the use of images in law, see the path-breaking study of Jennifer L. Mnookin, "The Image of Truth: Photographic Evidence and the Power of Analogy," in *Yale Journal of Law and the Humanities* 10, no. 1 (1998): 1–74; and Elizabeth G. Porter, "Taking Images Seriously," in *Columbia Law Review* 114, no. 7 (November 2014): 1687–1782.

6. Carlo Severi, *Le principe de la chimère: une anthropologie de la mémoire* (Paris : Editions Rue d'Ulm-Musée du quai Branly, 2007), 325; and "L'univers des

arts de la mémoire: Anthropologie d'un artefact mental," in *Annales: Histoire, Sciences Sociales*, no. 64 (2009): 491. See also, Carlos Severi, "Autorités sans auteurs: formes de l'autorité dans les traditions orales," in *De l'autorité*, ed. A. Compagnon (Paris: Odile Jacob, 2008), 93–123.

7. Cf. Peter Goodrich, *Legal Emblems and the Art of Law: Obiter Depicta as the Vision of Governance* (Cambridge University Press, 2014).

8. Earnes Elmo Calkins, *The Business of Advertising* (New York: D. Appleton, 1915), 9.

9. Ibid., 1–2.

10. Herbert Blumer, "Fashion: From Class Differentiation to Collective Selection," in *Sociological Quarterly* 10, no. 3 (1969): 275–91.

11. On customary law in ancient Rome, see Hans Rech's the classic study *Mos maiorum: Wesen und Wirkung der Tradition in Rom* (PhD diss., Philipps-Universität, Marburg, 1936). Following Pompeus Festus, "custom is an institute of the ancestors, that is, the memory of the ancients concerning above all religious practices and ceremonies" [Mos est institutum patrium, id est memoria veterum pertinens maxime ad religiones caerimoniasque antiquorum]: Advertising destroys and doesn't tolerate memory.

12. On the specific form of irony in advertising, see Leo Spitzer, "American Advertising Explained as Popular Art," in *Essays on English and American Literature* (Princeton, NJ: Princeton University Press, 1962): "And why does the advertiser, whose mouthpiece is the copywriter, allow himself to be presented before the public as a poet *malgre lui*? Surely it is because he feels himself protected, he feels the fanciful words of the advertisement protected, by invisible 'quotation marks' which can ward off the possible ridicule of the public and which exculpate him, in his own eyes, for his daring. By 'quotation marks' I mean to characterize an attitude toward language which is shared by the speaker and his public, and according to which he may use words with the implication: 'I have good reasons for saying this—but don't pin me down!' The public, for its part, reacts accordingly: there is on both sides a tacit understanding of the rules of the game (a game which also involves the necessary embellishment by the seller of his products and a corresponding attitude of sales-resistance on the part of the prospect). . . . Everyone knows that, while the advertised goods may be quite first-rate, the better world which the advertiser evokes is a never-never land. Nonetheless, the idealizations of advertising are not wasted upon the listener: though he cannot take up forthwith his dwelling in the paradisiac world filled with fragrant groves where golden fruit slowly ripen under the caress of the sun, his imagination has made the detour through this word-paradise and carries back the poetic flavor which will season the physical enjoyment of the orange-juice he will drink for breakfast the next morning. Here, in an unexpected corner of our technologically organized age, and in the service of the most highly rationalized

interests, poetry has developed its most miraculous quality: that of establishing a realm of pure, gratuitous, disinterested beauty, which has existence only in the imagination. And the poetic achievement is presented to the public with all sincerity—and with all cautiousness: with overtones of irony which preclude any too-serious commitment" (264–66).

13. Blumer, *Fashion*.

14. Arjun Appadurai, *Banking on Words. The Failure of Language in the Age of Derivative Finance* (Chicago: University of Chicago Press, 2015), 149ff.

1. WALLS

1. See Andre Leroi-Gourhan, *L'homme et la matière* (Paris: Albin Michel, 1943) and *L'art parietal: langage de la préhistoire* (Grenoble: Jérôme Millon, 1992).

2. Kevin Lynch, *The Image of the City* (Cambridge, MA: MIT Press, 1960).

3. This practice has not entirely disappeared: prices, measurements, and commercial regulations were inscribed on walls until the premodern era (the Duomo in Modena still preserves a trace of them), and even today it's on walls, often on chalkboards, that prices are displayed in bars. On signage, see the classic study of E. Fournier and J. Cousin, *Histoire des enseignes de Paris* (Paris: E. Dentu, 1884). On modern electric signs, see instead Philippe Artieres, *Les enseignes lumineuses: des écritures urbaines au XXè siècle* (Paris: Bayard, 2010).

4. "City walls are madmen's documents; Pompei's graffiti are the real tattoos of the walls." Cesare Lombroso, review of Alexandre Lacassagne, *Les tatouages: études anthropologiques et médico-légales, Archivio di psichiatria* II (1881).

5. See Allen Walker Read's lone, brilliant work, *Lexical Evidence from Epigraphy in Western North America: A Glossarial Study of the Low Elements in English Vocabulary* (Paris: private publication, 1935). On Pompei, see the excellent anthology curated by Vincent Hunink, *Glücklich ist dieser Ort! 1000 Graffiti aus Pompeji* (Stuttgart: Reclam, 2011). In Pompei, too, inscriptions often expressed a certain self-consciousness of the medium (see, for example, this chapter's epigraph).

6. We experience this with even the most mundane street signage—through them, every city duplicates itself, into a real body and its semiotic image. From a certain point of view, all cities are surreal spaces, bodies that literally cannot be identical to themselves. This is what Aragon understood when he made the city, in its most material and architectonic dimensions, the breeding ground of modern mythology.

7. It was Hannah Arendt who suggested identifying the public sphere with the space of appearance; see Arendt, *The Life of the Mind* (New York: Harcourt Brace Jovanovich, 1977). According to Barbara Carnevali, public space can be understood as a shared collective sensory organ, a *sensorium societatis*. See Barbara

Carnevali, *Le apparenze sociali. Una filosofia del prestigio* (Bologna: Il Mulino, 2012).

8. A vision of the city as the site of multiplying sensory experiences, and as a collective organ of perception, can also be found in Georg Simmel, "Die Gross-städte und das Geistesleben," in *Die Grossstadt. Vorträge und Aufsätze zur Städteausstellung*, ed. T. Petermann (Dresden: Jahrbuch der Gehe-Stiftung, 1903), 9:185–206; and in the artistic avant-garde of the 1930s. See, for example, Laszlo Moholy-Nagy, *Malerei, Fotographie, Film* (Mainz, Berlin: Kupferberg Verlag, 1967), 41.

9. On the genesis of the public sphere see Reiner Koselleck, *Critique and Crisis: Enlightenment and the Pathogenesis of Modern Society* (Cambridge, MA: MIT Press, 1988) and Jürgen Habermas, *The Structural Transformation of the Public Sphere* (Cambridge, MA: MIT Press, 1989).

10. With regards to Rome, it was Paul Zanker who first showed this. See Zanker, *Augustus und die Macht der Bilder* (Munich: H. Beck, 1987).

11. 1094a 20–1094b 10, in *Nicomachean Ethics*, trans. Terrence Irwin (Indianapolis, IN: Hackett Press, 1999), 2.

12. Hannah Arendt, *The Human Condition* (Chicago: University of Chicago Press, 1998); Jan Assmann, *Cultural Memory and Early Civilization: Writing, Remembrance, and Political Imagination* (Cambridge: Cambridge University Press, 2011); and Mary Douglas, *Leviticus as Literature* (Oxford: Oxford University Press, 1999).

13. See A. O. Hirschman, *The Passions and the Interests* (Princeton, NJ: Princeton University Press, 2013).

2. CITIES

1. Robert Park, *The City: Suggestions for the Investigation of Human Behavior in the Urban Environment* (Chicago: University of Chicago Press, 1984), 1.

2. See 1 Peter 2, 4–8; Ephesians 2, 19–22; Ignatius of Antioch, *Letters to the Ephesians* XI, 1, SC 10bis, 65–67 in *Apostolic Fathers*, vol. 1, ed. and trans. Bart D. Ehrman (Cambridge, MA: Harvard University Press Loeb Classical Library, 2004). See also *The Shepherd of Hermas,* in *Apostolic Fathers*, vol. 2, ed. and trans. Bart D. Ehrman (Cambridge, MA: Harvard University Press Loeb Classical Library, 2004).

3. On this topic see also the work of Marius Schneider, *Singende Steine: Rhythmus-Studien an 3 katalanischen Kreuzgängen ramnischen Stils* (Kassel and Basel: Bärenreiter Verlag, 1955); and Charles Malamoud's study *La danse des pierres, études sur la scène sacrificielle dans l'inde ancienne* (Paris: Le Seuil, 2005).

4. Marshall McLuhan's media theory is simply a radicalization of the idea of a symbolism immanent in every city. Not only do stones speak, in this view of

things, but all objects do, even or perhaps above all utilitarian ones. Things are not only symbols insofar as they're endowed with tangible external form and are thus objects of design. For McLuhan, every artifact is a medium. See McLuhan, *Understanding Media* (New York: McGraw-Hill, 1964).

5. Robert Venturi, Denise Scott Brown, and Steven Izenour were largely responsible for the invention of this category, in their epoch-making book's discussion of the famous "Big Duck"—the duck-shaped building on Long Island that contained a store selling ducks and duck eggs. See *Learning from Las Vegas: The Forgotten Symbolism of Architectural Forms* (Cambridge, MA: MIT Press, 1977). See also Robert Venturi and Denise Scott Brown, *Architecture as Signs and Systems: For a Mannerist Time* (Cambridge, MA: Belknap Press, 2004), 13–18.

6. On medieval architectonic symbolism, see the wonderful book by Joseph Sauer, *Symbolik des Kirchengebäudes und seiner Ausstattung in der Auffassung des Mittelalters*, rev. ed. (Freiburg im Breisgau: Herder, 1924).

7. Walter Benjamin, *The Arcades Project*, ed. Rolf Tiedemann, trans. Howard Eiland and Kevin McLaughlin (Cambridge, MA: Belknap Press, 2002), 24. For the most rigorous attempt to extend Benjamin's analysis of urban space, see Rem Koolhas, *Delirious New York: A Retroactive Manifesto for Manhattan* (New York: Monacelli Press, 1997).

8. Rayner Banham, *Los Angeles: The Architecture of Four Ecologies*, 2nd ed. (Berkeley: University of California Press, 2009), 121.

9. Venturi, Scott Brown, and Izenour, *Learning from Las Vegas*. See also Venturi and Brown, *Architecture as Signs and Systems*, 104.

10. Venturi, Scott Brown, and Izenour, *Learning from Las Vegas*, 104.

11. Ibid., 13: "Symbol dominates space . . . The sign is more important than the architecture. . . . Baroque domes were symbols as well as spatial constructions, and they are bigger in scale and higher outside than inside in order to dominate their urban setting and communicate their symbolic message."

12. Ibid.

13. Marshall McLuhan, *The Mechanical Bride: A Folklore of Industrial Man* (New York: Vanguard Press, 1951).

14. On the *sermo humilis* of local vernacular, see Venturi, Scott Brown, and Izenour, *Learning from Las Vegas*, 6.

15. On advertising as popular art form, see Leo Spitzer's excellent essay "American Advertising Explained as Popular Art," in *Essays on English and American Literature* (New York: Gordian Press, 1984), 248–77, especially p. 252: "But, at all times, there has existed, side by side with great art, that everyday art which the Germans have called *Gebrauchskunst* ('applied practical art'): that art which adorns the practical and the utilitarian with beauty. At no time has this type of art played so compensatory a role as is the case today, in the age of machinism, of rationalization, and of the subjection of man to the impersonal

necessities of social, economic, and political life. An emphasis on the beautiful has penetrated all levels of fabrication, down to mucilage bottles and matchbooks, and to the packaging of goods; it has also penetrating to the forms of propaganda used to advertise these goods."

16. This was the implicit lesson of Alois Riegl and the Vienna school. See Riegl, *The Late Roman Art Industry*, trans. Rolf Winkes (Rome: G. Bretschneider, 1985).

17. McLuhan, *Mechanical Bride*, v; see also ibid., 125–27.

18. For an analysis of this phenomenon, see William Pietz's wonderful *La fétiche: Généalogie d'un problème* (Paris: Kargo/L'Eclat, 2005). See also his essay "Fetishism and Materialism: The Limits of Theory in Marx," in *Fetishism as Cultural Discourse*, ed. Emily Apter and William Pietz (Ithaca, NY: Cornell University Press, 1993), 119–51.

19. Karl Marx, *Capital*, trans. Ben Fowkes (New York: Vintage Books, 1977), 1:165.

20. Marx, *Capital*, 1:164–65.

21. See Jean Baudrillard, *The System of Objects,* trans. James Benedict (New York: Verso, 1996), and *For a Critique of the Political Economy of the Sign*, trans. Charles Levin (St. Louis, MO: Telos Press, 1981).

22. Marx, *Capital*, 1:163.

3. THE BANALITY OF THE GOOD

1. "I don't know what it can mean / that I am so sad, / a fairy-tale from ancient times, / which I can't get out of my mind."

2. This is the idea behind Howard S. Becker's excellent book *Telling about Society* (Chicago: University of Chicago Press, 2007).

3. This idea is expressed by one of the founding fathers of modern advertising, Ernest Dichter, in his *Handbook of Consumers' Motivations: The Psychology of the World of Objects* (New York: McGraw-Hill, 1964). Discussing modern Western man, Dichter writes, "his customs, motivations, desires, and hopes are often not too far removed from the rituals and fetishes of the New Guineans"—the latter "carve their fetishes out of the skulls of their enemies," while the former simply buy them in supermarkets (v–vi).

4. Gianluigi Simonetti argues this in "La letteratura come spot," *Contemporanea*, no. 8 (2010): 15–27, referring to Alessandro Baricco's concept of "sistema passante" [transitory system]; see Baricco, *I barbari* (Milano: Feltrinelli Editore, 2009). On this same issue, see also Judith Williamson, *Decoding Advertisements: Ideology and Meaning in Advertising* (London and New York: Marion Boyars, 1978).

5. Rudolf Wittkower, *Allegory and the Migration of Symbols* (London: Thames and Hudson, 1977).

6. Although it can migrate in space, advertising seems completely incapable of travelling in time; the rate at which symbols become obsolete seems unbelievably fast in the case of advertising communication.

7. See Martha Nussbaum, *Poetic Justice: The Literary Imagination and Public Life* (Boston, MA: Beacon Press, 1995) and *Love's Knowledge: Essays on Philosophy and Literature* (Oxford: Oxford University Press, 1992).

8. In addition to Nussbaum's *Poetic Justice*, see also Stanley Cavell, *The Claim of Reason: Wittgenstein, Skepticism, Morality, and Tragedy* (Oxford: Oxford University Press, 1999); Vincent Descombes, *Proust: Philosophy of the Novel*, trans. Catherine Chance Macksey (Stanford, CA: Stanford University Press, 1992); Jacques Bouveresse, *La connaissance de l'écrivain: Sur la littérature* (Marseille: Agone, 2008); and Barbara Carnevali, "Mimésis littéraire et connaissance morale: la tradition de l'"éthopée," *Annales HSS*, no. 2 (2010): 291–324.

9. This idea of advertising realism is developed in Michael Schudon, *Advertising, the Uneasy Persuasion: Its Dubious Impact on American Society* (New York: Basic Books, 1986).

10. Cicero, *Tusculan Disputations*, trans. C. D. Yonge (New York: Harper and Bros, 1877), V.iv.10. See also *Academica* I.iv.15.

11. Aristotle, *Metaphysics*, trans. Hugh Tredennick (Cambridge, MA: Harvard University Press, 1933/1989), 987b2.

12. Plato, *The Republic*, trans. Benjamin Jowett (New York: Modern Library, 1941), 508c.

13. Ibid., 508e.

14. Ibid., 509b.

15. Ibid., 505a.

16. Ibid., 509b.

17. Ibid., 504e.

18. Aristotle, *Nicomachean Ethics* in *Aristotle in 23 Volumes*, vol. 19, trans. H. Rackham (Cambridge, MA: Harvard University Press, 1934), 1.6.14.

19. Plotinus, *Enneads*, ed. John Dillon, trans. Stephan MacKenna (New York: Penguin, 1991), VI.7.27.

20. Ibid. Cf. Hans-Georg Gadamer, *The Idea of the Good in Platonic-Aristotelian Philosophy*, trans. P. Christopher Smith (New Haven, CT: Yale University Press, 1986).

21. As the subtitle of a famous medieval treatise reminds us, Boethius's *De hebdomadibus*, this is always a question of understanding "how substances may be good from the fact of their existence, although they are not substantial goods." On this treatise, see also Claudio Micaelli, *Dion el pensiero di Boezio* (Naples: M. D'Auria, 1995); on its premises, see Ernst Benz, *Marius Victorinus und die Entwicklung der abendländischen Willensmetaphysik* (Stuttgart: Kohlhammer, 1932).

22. For a critical history of the last century of this transformation, see Victoria De Grazia, *Irresistible Empire: America's Advance Through Twentieth-Century Europe* (Cambridge, MA: Belknap Press of Harvard University Press, 2005).

23. On the affirmation of ordinary life in modernity see the brilliant analyses of Charles Taylor in *Sources of the Self: The Making of the Modern Identity* (Cambridge: Cambridge University Press, 1989), especially chap. 13.

24. On the consequences of this in the literary sphere, see Guido Mazzoni, *Teoria del romanzo* (Bologna: Il Mulino, 2011).

25. This is the thesis of Ernst Kapp's famous book *Grundlinien einer Philosophie der Technik* (Braunschweig: George Westermann, 1877). Starting from the intuition that "every action completed with the aid of a tool originates in an organic movement" (62–63), Kapp advances the argument that every tool is "the real prolongation [*Forsetzung*] of the organism and the external transposition of the interior world" (26), the formal projection of a body organ.

26. Among the many articulations of this principle, see F. Sigaut, *Comment Homo devint faber* (Paris: CNRS Editions, 2012), 118.

27. Charles Larmore, *Patterns of Moral Complexity* (Cambridge: Cambridge University Press, 1987), 138.

28. Ibid.

29. Charles Larmore, *The Practices of the Self*, trans. Sharon Bowman (Chicago: University of Chicago Press, 2010), 176.

30. Larmore, *Practices of the Self*, 178.

31. Ibid., 179.

4. TOTEM

1. Charles de Brosses, *Du culte des dieux Fétiches* (Geneva: Cramer, 1760), 18, translated by Daniel Leonard as "On the Worship of the Fetish Gods: Or, A Parallel of the Ancient Religion of Egypt with the Present Religion of Nigritia," in Rosalind C. Morris and Daniel H. Leonard, *The Returns of Fetishism: Charles de Brosses and the Afterlives of an Idea; With a New Translation of "On the Worship of the Fetish Gods"* (Chicago: University of Chicago Press, 2016), 44–132.

2. de Brosses, *Du culte*, 19.

3. See Pietze, *Le fétiche*, ch. 4, "Charles de Brosses et la théorie du fétichisme," 117–40.

4. "I ask that I be permitted to use this expression ["fetishism"] habitually: though in its proper signification it refers in particular to the beliefs of African Negroes, I signal in advance that I plan to use it equally in speaking of any other nation whatsoever, where the objects of worship are animals, or inanimate beings that are divinized. I will sometimes use it even in talking about certain peoples for whom objects of this sort are not so much Gods, properly speaking, as they

are things endowed with a divine virtue: oracles, amulets, and protective talismans. For in general, all these ways of thinking have at bottom the same source, which is merely the appurtenance of a general Religion spread very far over the entire earth, and which must be examined on its own as composing a particular class among the diversity of Pagan Religions, all of them rather different among themselves" (de Broses, "On the Worship of the Fetish Gods," 45–46).

5. Pietz, *Le fétiche*, 118.

6. The literature on the history of this concept in the humanities and social sciences is vast. See Alfonso M. Ianoco, *Teorie del feticismo: Il problema filosofico e storico di un immenso malinteso"* (Milano: Giuffré, 1985); Andrea Borsari, ed., *L'esperienza delle cose* (Genova: Marietti, 1992); Karl-Heinz Kohl, *Die Macht der Dinge: Geschichte und Theorie sakraler Objekte* (München: C. H. Beck, 2003); and Frederic Keck, "Fiction, folie, fétichisme: Claude Lévi-Strauss entre Comte et *La Comédie humaine*," *L'Homme*, nos. 175/176 (2005): 203–18. For a concise review of the use of fetishism in contemporary art, see Massimo Fusillo, *Feticci. Letteratura, cinema, arti visive* (Bologna: Il Mulino, 2012).

7. Saint Augustine, *On Christian Doctrine,* trans. J. F. Shaw (New York: Dover Philosophical Classics, 2009), 3. On this distinction, see Hannah Arendt, *Love and Saint Augustine*, ed. Joanna Vechiarelli Scott (Chicago: University of Chicago Press, 1996); R. Canning, "The Augustinian uti/frui Distinction in the Relation between Love for Neighbour and Love for God," *Augustiniana* 33 (1983): 165–231; Christian Gnilka, *Der Begriff des "rechten Gebrauchs"* (Basel/Stuttgart: Schwabe Verlag, 1984); Alavaro Grion, "La 'fruizione' nella storia della teologia," *Sapienza* 17 (1964): 186–216, 337–50; Rudolf Lorenz, "Fruitio Dei bei Augustin," *Zeitschrift für Kirchengeschichte* 63 (1950/51): 75–132; Georg Pfligersdorffer, "Zu den Grundlagen des augustinischen Begriffspaares uti-frui," *Augustino praeceptori: Gesammelte Aufsätze zu Augustinus*, ed. K. Forstner and M. Fussl (Salzburg: Abakus Verlag, 1987), 101–31.

8. Augustine, *On Christian Doctrine,* 4.

9. Ibid.

10. "If this object impassions you it is because within, hidden in it, there is the object of desire, *agalma*." Jacques Lacan, *Le Séminaire, Livre VIII, Le transfert* (Paris: Editions du Seuil, 1991), 180. On the partial object and the object *a*, see also Slavoj Žižek, *The Fragile Absolute or Why is the Christian Legacy Worth Fighting For* (London: Verso, 2000) and Guy le Gaufey, *L'objet a, Approches de l'invention de Lacan* (Paris: Epel, 2012). Augustine's influence on Freud and Lacan (mediated also, in the case of the latter, by the Jansenist tradition) remains largely to be assessed.

11. It would be impossible to adequately review them here. This notion wholly inspired the reflections of Baudrillard in *The System of Objects* and *For a Critique*

of the Political Economy of the Sign; and of Pierre Bourdieu, *Distinction: A Social Critique of the Judgement of Taste*, trans. Richard Nice (Cambridge, MA: Harvard University Press, 1984). Roland Barthes's foundational work, however, is more original; see Barthes, *Mythologies*, trans. Annette Lavers (New York: Hill and Wang, 1972).

12. de Brosses, *Du culte*, 18.

13. Marx, *Capital*, 163–64.

14. Marshall Sahlins, "La Pensée Bourgeoise: Western Society as Culture," in *Culture in Practice: Selected Essays* (New York: Zone Books, 2000), 167.

15. Ibid.

16. Ibid., 175.

17. Ibid., 166.

18. Baudrillard, *For a Critique of the Political Economy of the Sign*, 37.

19. Sahlins, "La Pensée Bourgeoise," 175: "It is by their meaningful differences from other goods that objects are rendered exchangeable: they thus become use-values to certain persons, who are correspondingly differentiated from other subjects. At the same time, as a modular construction of concrete elements combined by human invention, manufactured goods uniquely lend themselves to this type of discourse. Fashioning the product, man does not merely alienate his labor, congealed thus in objective form, but by the physical modification he effects he sediments a thought. The object stands as a human concept outside itself, as man speaking to man through the medium of things."

20. Baudrillard is particularly relevant here; he writes in *For a Critique of the Political Economy of the Sign*, 63–64: "The empirical 'object,' given in its contingency of form, color, material, function and discourse (or, if it is a cultural object, in its aesthetic finality) is a myth. How often it has been wished away! But the object is *nothing*. It is nothing but the different types of relations and significations that converge, contradict themselves, and twist around it, as such—the hidden logic that not only arranges this bundle of relations, but directs the manifest discourse that overlays and occludes it. . . . Insofar as I make use of a refrigerator as a machine, it is not an object. It is a refrigerator. Talking about refrigerators or automobiles in terms of 'objects' is something else. That is, it has nothing to do with them in their 'objective' relation to keeping things cold or transportation. It is to speak of the object as functionally decontextualized . . . as an object specified by its trademark, charged with differential connotations of status, prestige and fashion. *This* is the 'object of consumption.' It can just as easily be a vase as a refrigerator, or, for that matter, a whoopee cushion. Properly speaking, it has no more existence than a phoneme has an absolute meaning in linguistics."

21. Marshall Sahlins, "La Pensée Bourgeoise: Western Society as Culture," 175: "the bourgeois totemism in other words, is potentially more elaborate than any

wild variety, not that it has been liberated from a natural-material basis, but precisely because nature has been domesticated"; "The clothing system in particular replicates for Western society the functions of the so-called totemism" (194); even gastronomy seems to be "an entire totemic order, uniting in a parallel series of differences the status of persons and what they eat" (173).

22. Thorstein Veblen, *Theory of the Leisure Class: An Economic Study of Institutions* (New York: Macmillan, 1899).

23. With a few obvious differences, this performative contradiction is analogous to the one revealed by Latour in relation to the modern constitution and the separation between nature and culture. See Latour, *We Have Never Been Modern*, trans. Catherine Porter (Cambridge, MA: Harvard University Press, 1993).

24. Alfred Gell, *Art and Agency. An Anthropological Theory* (Oxford: Oxford University Press, 1998), 16.

25. Ibid., 6: "In place of symbolic communication, I place all the emphasis on *agency, intention, causation, result*, and *transformation*. I view art as a system of action, intended to change the world rather than encode symbolic propositions about it. The 'action'-centred approach to art is inherently more anthropological than the alternative semiotic approach because it is preoccupied with the practical mediatory role of art objects in the social process, rather than with the interpretation of objects 'as if' they were texts."

26. Ibid., 8–9.

27. On art institutionalizing a way of relating to things, see Carlo Severi, "Autorité sans auteur: formes de l'autorité dans les traditions orales" in *De l'autorité*, ed. Antoine Compagnon (Paris: Odile Jacob, 2008), 93–123. On the theological construction of the exceptional status of the artistic object, see the works of Etienne Anheim, "Expertise et construction de la valeur artistique dans la peinture toscane (XIe–XVe siècle)," *Revue de Synthèse: L'expertise artistique* 1, no. 132/6 (2011): 11–31; and Anheim, "Lo sagrado en el mundo. La cultura corte-sana del siglo XIV y suproyecciòn," in *Modelos culturales y normas sociales al final de la Edad Media*, ed. Patrick Boucheron and Francisco Ruiz Gòmez (Madrid and La Mancha: Ediciones de la Universidad de Castilla-La Mancha, 2009), 311–30.

28. Gell, *Art and Agency*, 123: "We certainly do not have to postulate a particular 'mentality' (primitive, uncritical, gullible, etc.) to account for idolatry; the worship of images is compatible with an extreme degree of philosophical and critical acumen, as the example of textual Hinduism amply demonstrates, besides numerous treatises on 'theurgy' (the creation of gods) from classical antiquity."

29. Karl Marx, *Ökonomisch-Philosophische Manusckripte* (Frankfurt am Main: Suhrkamp, 2009), 89–91. English edition in Marx, *Early Writings*, trans. Rodney Livingstone and Gregor Benton (New York: Penguin Books, 1975).

30. See the profound reflections of Gotthard Günther, *Das Bewusstsein der Maschinen. Eine Metaphysik der Kypernetik* (Baden-Baden: AGIS Verlag, 1957), and the extremely important book by Fabian Ludueña Romandini, *La comunidad de los espectros. I. Antropotecnia* (Buenos Aires: Miño y Davila, 2010).

31. On design, the industrial arts, and their place in the system of traditional arts, see Maurizio Vitta, *Il rifiuto degli dei: Teoria delle belle arti industriali* (Torino: Einaudi, 2012), and Vitta, *Il progetto della bellezza: Il design tra arte e tecnica dal 1851 a oggi* (Torino: Einaudi, 2011). For a social history of design, see instead Adrian Forty, *Objects of Desire: Design and Society Since 1750* (London: Thames and Hudson, 1986).

32. "There should be no such thing as art divorced from life, with beautiful things to look at and hideous things to use. If what we use every day is made with art, and not thrown together by chance or caprice, then we shall have nothing to hide." Bruno Munari, *Design as Art*, trans. Patrick Creagh (New York: Penguin, 1971), 19. Munari is explicitly referring to Gropius's Bauhaus manifesto. See also Munari, *Artista e designer* (Roma and Bari: Laterza, 1971).

33. Ibid.

34. Gustave Flaubert, Letter to Louise Colet, *Correspondance, Juillet 1851–Décembre 1858* (Paris: Gallimard, 1980), 483–84.

35. The secondary literature on this is by now vast. Besides the classic by André Morize, *L'Apologie du luxe au XVIIIe siècle et le Mondain de Voltaire* (Paris: H. Didier, 1909), see the more recent studies by Maxime Berg and Helen Clifford, eds., *Consumers and Luxury: Consumer Culture in Europe 1650–1850* (Manchester: Manchester University Press, 1999); Maxine Berg and Elisabet Eger, eds., *Luxury in the Eighteenth Century: Debates, Desires and Delectable Goods* (Basingstoke: Palgrave, 2003). For an important historical context, see also Daniel Roche, *La culture des apparences: Une histoire du vêtement (XVIIe–XVIIIe siècle)* (Paris: Fayard, 1989). For its afterlife, see R. H. *Williams, Dream Worlds: Mass Consumption in Late Nineteenth Century France* (Berkeley: University of California Press, 1992); W. G. Breckman, "Disciplining Consumption: The Debate about Luxury in Wilhelmine Germany 1890–1914," *Journal of Social History*, no. 24 (1990): 485–505. For a more wide-ranging discussion of luxury see Olivier Assouly, ed., *Le luxe: Essais sur la fabrique de l'ostentation* (Paris: IFM-Editions du Regard, 2011). As early as the beginning of the last century, Werner Sombart referred to this same debate to demonstrate that it is the love of things and commodities and luxury (derived from a profound transformation of affective relationships in the West beginning in the Late Middle Ages) that generated capitalism. See Sombart, *Luxus und Kapitalismus (Studien zur Entwicklungsgeschichte des modernen Kapitalismus)* (Munich and Leipzig: Duncker and Humblot, 1912). Peter Sloterdijk arrived at conclusions similar to Sombart's about the relationship between capitalism, luxury, and the affective order (albeit by outlining a different

genealogy); see Sloterdijk, *Sphären III: Schäume, Plurale Sphärologie* (Frankfurt am Main: Suhrkamp, 2004).

36. Jean Jacques Rousseau, *Social Contact and Discourses*, trans. G. D. H. Cole (New York: E. P. Dutton and Co., 1913).

37. Among countless examples one might cite the studies of Georget Ritzer, *Enchanting a Disenchanted World: Revolutionizing the Means of Consumption* (Thousand Oaks, CA: Pine Forge Press, 1999) and *The McDonaldization of Society* (Thousand Oaks, CA: Sage Publications, 1993).

38. David Hume, "Of Refinement in the Arts," *Selected Essays*, ed. Stephen Copley and Andrew Edgard (Oxford: Oxford University Press, 2008), 170. The modern leader of this new *querelle sur le luxe* is, of course, Guy Debord, *Society of the Spectacle* (Kalamazoo, MI: Black and Red, 2000). We tend, however, to forget this book's roots in an older tradition. Many of these ideas about the alienation belonging to the "society of the image" had already been expressed in the famous book by Daniel J. Boorstin, *The Image: A Guide to Pseudoevents in America* (New York: Atheneum, 1962). The notion of "spectacle" comes rather from Jules de Gaultier, *La sensibilité metaphysique* (Paris: Librarie F. Alcan, 1928).

39. The eighteenth-century participants in this debate were also aware of this. "All of the Latin classics, whom we peruse in our infancy, are full of these sentiments, and universally ascribe the ruin of their state to the arts and riches imported from the East; insomuch, that Sallus represents a taste for painting as a vice, no less than lewdness and drinking." Hume, "Of Refinement in the Arts," 173.

40. Jean-François de Saint-Lambert, "Luxury," *The Encyclopedia of Diderot and d'Alembert Collaborative Translation Project*, trans. Claude Blanchi (Ann Arbor: University of Michigan Library, 2003), accessed 2 March 2015, http://hdl .handle.net/2027/spo.did2222.0000.048. Originally published as "Luxe," *Encyclopédie ou Dictionnaire raisonné des sciences, des arts et des métiers*, vol. 9 (Paris, 1765).

41. This is the position that will guide Ernst Bloch's *summa*; see Bloch, *The Principle of Hope*, trans. Neville Plaice, Stephen Plaice, and Paul Knight (Cambridge, MA: MIT Press, 1986).

5. THE WORLD OF THINGS

1. Aristotle, *Nicomachean Ethics*, 1096.8.

2. Antoine de Montchrestien, *Traicté de l'oeconomie politique*, ed. T. Funck-Brentano (Paris: Librairie Plon, 1889), 99: "le bonheur des hommes . . . consiste principalement en la richesse, et la richesse dans le travail." On Montchrestien see Alain Guery, *Montchrestien et Cantillon: Le commerce et l'émergence d'une pensée économique* (Paris: ENS Editions, 2011).

3. Max Weber, *The Protestant Work Ethic and the Spirit of Capitalism*, trans. Peter Baehr and Gordon C. Wells (New York: Penguin Books, 2002); and Charles Taylor, *Sources of the Self* (Cambridge, MA: Harvard University Press, 1989).

4. Gregory's famous formulation can be found in epistle 13 to the bishop Serenus of Marseille: "Nam quod legentibus scriptura, hoc idiotis praestat pictura cernentibus, quia in ipsa etiam ignorantes vident quid sequi debeant, in ipsa legunt qui litteras nesciunt" (PL 77, c. 1128). On the relationship between writing and iconography in the medieval period, and on historical prejudices regarding it, see the important works of Jerome Baschet, *L'iconographie médiévale* (Paris: Gallimard, 2008).

5. Leo Spitzer first highlighted this point in "American Advertising Explained as Popular Art." On emblematic literature, see Karl Gielow, "Die Hieroglyphen-kunde des Humanismus in der Allegorie der Renaissance," *Jahrbuch der Kunsthistorischen Sammlungen des Allerhöchsten Kaiserhauses* 32 (1915): 1–232; Anne-Elisabeth Spica, *Symbolique humaniste et emblématique: l'évolution et les genres (1580–1700)* (Paris: Honoré Champion éditeur, 1966); and Arthur Henkel and Albrecht Schöne, *Emblemata. Handbuch zur Sinnbildkunst des XVI. und XVII. Jahrhunderts* (Stuttgart: Weimar, 1967).

6. Eric Michaud, "Le mythe social ou l'efficacité de l'image sans images," *Mil neuf cent. Revue d'histoire intellectuelle*, no. 28 (2010): 173–83. Michaud leans on the scholarship of the early twentieth century, such as Harry L. Hollingworth, *Advertising and Selling: Principles of Appeal and Response* (New York: Appleton and Company, 1913), and Octave-Jacques Gerin and Charles Espinadel, *La publicité suggestive: Théorie et technique* (Paris: H. Dunod et E. Pinat, 1911).

7. This notion is quite widespread in modern thought. See Bernard Mandeville, *The Fable of the Bees*, ed. F. B. Kaye (Indianapolis, IN: Liberty Fund, 1988), Remark L: "what is call'd superfluous to some degree of People, will be thought requisite to those of higher Quality; and neither the World nor the Skill of Man can produce any thing so curious or extravagant, but some most Gracious Sovereign or other, if it either eases or diverts him, will reckon it among the Necessaries of Life."

8. See Williamson, *Decoding Advertisements*. As Gianluigi Simonetti has shown (in "La letteratura come spot"), literature seems to have assimilated this principle to the point that it proposes prosopographies based not on psychology but on a simple listing of commodities employed. The author calls this procedure "*abbreviazione merceologica*" (abbreviation by means of commodities).

9. There's an extensive literature on the moral or religious meaning of advertising. See T. J. Jackson Lears, "From Salvation to Self-Realization: Advertising and the Therapeutic Roots of the Consumer Culture, 1880–1930," in *The Culture of Consumption: Critical Essays in American History, 1880–1980*, ed.

R. Wightman Fox and T. J. Jackson Lears (New York: Pantheon Books, 1983), 1–38; Stephen Fox, *The Mirror Makers: A History of American Advertising and Its Creators* (Chicago: University of Illinois Press, 1984); and T. J. Jackson Lears, *Fables of Abundances: A Cultural History of Advertising in America* (New York: Basic Books, 1994).

10. John Locke, *Second Treatise on Government*, ed. C. B. McPherson (Indianapolis, IN: Hackett Publishing Company, 1980), V.42.

11. Ibid.

12. Locke, *Second Treatise*, V.28.

13. Adam Smith, *An Inquiry into the Causes of the Wealth of Nations*, ed. Edwin Cannan (London: Metheun, 1904), I.V.1: "The value of any commodity, therefore, to the person who possesses it, and who means not to use or consume it himself, but to exchange it for other commodities, is equal to the quantity of labour which it enables him to purchase or command." The secondary literature on the history of the concept of value is immense. See, for example, Hannah Robie Sewall, "The Theory of Value before Adam Smith," *Publications of the American Economic Association*, no. 2 (1901): 1–128; Maurice Dobb, *Theories of Value and Distribution Since Adam Smith: Ideology and Economic Theory* (Cambridge: Cambridge University Press, 1973); Odd Langholm, *Price and Value in the Aristotelian Tradition: A Study in Scholastic Economic Sources* (Bergen: Universitetsforlaget, 1979); Langholm, *Economics in the Medieval Schools: Wealth, Exchange, Value, Money, and Usury according to the Paris Theological Tradition 1200–1350* (Leyde: E. J. Brill, 1992); Joseph Schumpeter, *Histoire de l'analyse économique* (Paris: Gallimard, 1983); Jean Claude Perrot, *Une histoire intellectuelle de l'économie politique, XVIe–XVIIIe siècle* (Paris: Éditions de l'École des Hautes Études en Sciences Sociales, 1992); Sylvain Piron, "Albert le Grand et le concept de valeur," in *I beni di questo mondo: Teorie etico-economiche nel laboratorio dell'Europa medievale*, ed. R. Lambertini and L. Sileo (Atti del Convegno della Società Italiana per lo Studio del Pensiero Medievale, Rome, September 19–21, 2005). For a critical overview of the theory of value in current doctrine, see André Orléan, *L'empire de la valeur: Réfonder l'économie* (Paris: Editions du Seuil, 2011).

14. Karl Marx, *A Contribution to the Critique of Political Economy*, trans. N. I. Stone (Chicago: Charles H. Kerr, 1904).

15. Georg Simmel, *The Philosophy of Money*, trans. Tom Bottomore and David Frisby (New York: Routledge Classics, 1978, 2011).

16. Simmel, *Philosophy of Money*, 106.

17. Arjun Appadurai, "Introduction: Commodities and Politics of Value," in *The Social Life of Things*, ed. Appadurai (Cambridge: Cambridge University Press, 1986), 6: "I shall suggest that commodities are things with a particular type of

social potential, that they are distinguishable from products, objects, goods, artifacts, and other sorts of things, but only in certain respects and from a certain point of view."

18. Appadurai, "Introduction," 13, criticized "an excessively positivist conception of the commodity, as being a certain kind of thing, thus restricting the debate to the matter of deciding what kind of thing it is." A commodity should rather be seen as "a thing in a certain situation, a situation that can characterize many different sorts of things, at different points in their social life."

19. Ibid.: "I propose that the commodity situation in the social life of any thing be defined as the situation in which its exchangeability (past, present, or future) for some other thing is its socially relevant feature."

20. Appadurai, "Introduction," 17: "[T]he commodity phase of the life history of an object does not exhaust its biography; it is culturally regulated; and its interpretation is open to individual manipulation to some degree. . . . But the important point is that the commodity is not one kind of thing rather than another, but one phase in the life of some things."

21. This is the argument of Mary Douglas and Baron Isherwood's extremely important book, *The World of Good: Towards an Anthropology of Consumption* (London: Routledge, 1996).

22. Douglas and Isherwood, *World of Good*, 37. Dick Hebdige, in *Subculture: The Meaning of Style* (London: Routledge, 1979), further showed how, beginning in the 1960s, the construction of subcultural identities was entirely defined by a certain way of relating to commodities.

23. This is Daniel Miller's thesis in his brilliant book *The Comfort of Things* (Cambridge: Polity Press, 2008). Miller's work has revolutionized the anthropology of consumption. See, for starters, *Material Culture and Mass Consumption* (Oxford: Basil Blackwell, 1987); *A Theory of Shopping* (Cambridge: Polity Press/ Cornell University Press, 1998); and *Consumption* (London: Routledge, 2001).

24. See the famous reflections of Wilhelm Dilthey, *The Formation of the Historical World in the Human Sciences*, ed. Rudolf A. Makkreel and Frithjof Rodi (Princeton, NJ: Princeton University Press, 2002); and Georg Simmel, "The Concept and Tragedy of Culture," in *Simmel on Culture*, ed. David Frisby and Mike Featherstone (London: Sage, 1997). For a study of this Diltheyan category, see also Remo Bodei, *La vita delle cose* (Roma-Bari: Laterza, 2009), to which this book owes much more than these notes can express.

25. This is one of the teachings of Fernand Braudel and his school: "how can one imagine the history of Europe without its domesticated animals, its plows, its hitches, its carts?" Braudel, *La dynamique du capitalisme* (Paris: Flammarion, 2008), 18. See also Braudel, *Capitalism and Material Life, 1400–1800* (New York: Harper Collins, 1973); Daniel Roche, *A History of Everyday Things: The Birth of Consumption in France, 1600–1800*, trans. Brian Pearce (Cambridge: Cambridge

University Press, 2000); Guy Thuillier, *Pour une histoire du quotidien au XIX siècle* (Paris: Mouton, 1977); and Frank Trentmann, *Empire of Things: How We Became a World of Consumers, Fifteenth Century to the Twenty-First* (London: Allen Lane/Penguin; New York: HarperCollins 2016).

26. Marie-Angèle Hermitte, in discussing native populations, speaks of "sovereign goods," meaning things that convey and embody the sovereignty of a community that does not exist outside the relation to reality that this sovereignty embodies. See Hermitte, "Les revendications des autochtones sur leurs ressources et leurs connaissances Economie du partage ou biens souverains," in *La bioéquité: Batailles autour du partage du vivant*, ed. F. Bellivier and Ch. Noiville (Paris: Autrement, 2009), 115–35.

27. Plutarch, *Romulus* 11, 1–4; Ovid, *Fasti* 4, 821–24. See also Georges Dumezil, *La religione romana arcaica* (Milano: BUR, 2001), 310; and Georg Wissow, *Religion und Kultus der Römer* (Munich: C. H. Beck, 1971), 234.

28. This has been a commonplace in economic thought since its beginnings and has been widely taken up in philosophical scholarship as well. See, for example, Dudley North, "Discourses about Trade," in *A Select Collection of Early English Tracts on Commerce from the Originals of Mun, Roberts, North, and Others*, ed. John Ramsay McCullouch (London: Printed for the Political Economy Club, 1856), 514: "That the whole World as to Trade, is but as one Nation or People."

29. *Natural History*, ed. G. P. Goold (Cambridge, MA: Harvard University Press Loeb Classical Library, 1938), vol. 330, II.3.4 (175).

30. Aetius, *Placita Philosophorum* II.1.1, in Herman Diels, *Fragmente der Vorsokratiker*, ed. Walther Kranz (Hildesheim: Weidmannsche Verlagsbuchhandlung, 2004), 14 A 21.

31. Alexander von Humboldt, *Kosmos: Entwurf einer physischen Weltbeschreibung* (Darmstadt: Wissenschaftliche Buchgesellschaft, 1993 [1845]), 1:52. For a history of this notion, see the extremely dense volumes by Walter Kranz, *Kosmos: Archiv für Begriffsgeschichte*, 2:1–2 (Bonn: 1955–57); and, less recent but perhaps more interesting, Gustave-Adolphe Kreiss, *Sur le sens du mot cosmos dans le Nouveau Testament* (Strasbourg: n.p., 1837).

32. Plato, *Lysis, Symposium, Gorgias*, trans. W. R. M. Lamb (Cambridge, MA: Harvard University Press Loeb Classical Library, 1925), vol. 166, 506e.

33. Plato, *Timaeus, Critias, Cleitophon, Menexenus, Epistles*, trans. R. G. Bury (Cambridge, MA: Harvard University Press Loeb Classical Library, 1925), vol. 234, 30a (53).

6. TOWARD A MORAL HYPERREALISM

1. In addition to the sociology of Talcott Parsons, see Niklas Luhmann, *Theory of Society* (Stanford, CA: Stanford University Press, 2012), and *The Reality of Mass*

Media (Cambridge: Polity Press, 2000); Jürgen Habermas, *The Theory of Communicative Action* (Boston, MA: Beacon Press, 1984); Ulrich Beck, *Risk Society: Towards a New Modernity* (Newbury Park, CA: Sage Publications, 1992); Scott Lash, "Reflexive Modernization: The Aesthetic Dimension" in *Theory, Culture and Society*, no. 10 (1993): 1–23; Anthony Giddens, *The Consequences of Modernity* (Stanford, CA: Stanford University Press, 1990); and Ulrich Beck, Anthony Giddens, and Scott Lash, *Reflexive Modernization: Politics, Tradition and Aesthetics In the Modern Social Order* (Cambridge: Polity Press, 1994).

2. See Habermas, *Structural Transformation* and *Theory of Communicative Action*, and Michael Walzer, *Spheres of Justice: A Defense of Pluralism and Equality* (New York: Basic Books, 1983).

3. See the works of Giacomo Todeschini, *Franciscan Wealth: From Voluntary Poverty to Market Society* (Saint Bonaventure, NY: Franciscan Institute, Saint Bonaventure University, 2009); Sylvain Piron, "Les mouvements chrétiens de pauvreté au Moyen Âge central," in *Sobriété volontaire: en quête de nouveaux modes de vie*, ed. D. Bourg and P. Roch (Geneva: Fides et labor, 2012), 49–73; and Piron's extremely edition of Peter of John Olivi, *Traité des contrats* (Paris: Les Belles-Lettres, 2012).

4. See Walter Benjamin, "Unpacking My Library: A Talk About Book Collecting," in *Illuminations*, ed. Hannah Arendt, trans. Harry Zohn (New York: Schocken, 1978), 59–68, and the classic work by Krzysztof Pomian, *Collectors and Curiosities: Paris and Venice, 1500–1800* (Cambridge, UK: Polity, 1990). See also Susan M. Pearce, *Interpreting Objects and Collections* (London: Routledge, 1994).

5. See Pier-Paolo Portinaro, *Il realismo politico* (Roma-Bari: Laterza, 2002).

6. For a metaphysical translation of this principle, see the reflections of Markus Gabriel, *Fields of Sense: A New Realist Ontology* (Edinburgh: Edinburgh University Press, 2015); Gabriel, *Why the World Does Not Exist* (Cambridge, UK: Polity Press, 2015); and Maurizio Ferraris, *Introduction to New Realism*, trans. Sarah de Sanctis (London: Bloomsbury, 2015).

7. Baruch Spinoza, *A Political Treatise*, trans. R. H. M. Elwes (New York: Cosimo Classics, 2007), 287: "Philosophers conceive of the passions which harass us as vices into which men fall by their own fault, and, therefore, generally deride, bewail, or blame them, or execrate them, if they wish to seem unusually pious. And so they think they are doing something wonderful, and reaching the pinnacle of learning, when they are clever enough to bestow manifold praise on such human nature, as is nowhere to be found, and to make verbal attacks on that which, in fact, exists. For they conceive of men, not as they are, but as they themselves would like them to be. Whence it has come to pass that, instead of ethics, they have generally written satire, and that they have never conceived a theory of politics, which could be turned to use, but such as might be taken for a

chimera, or might have been formed in Utopia, or in that golden age of the poets when, to be sure, there was least need of it. Accordingly, as in all sciences, which have a useful application, so especially in that of politics, theory is supposed to be at variance with practice; and no men are esteemed less fit to direct public affairs than theorists or philosophers."

COMMONALITIES
Timothy C. Campbell, series editor

Roberto Esposito, *Terms of the Political: Community, Immunity, Biopolitics.* Translated by Rhiannon Noel Welch. Introduction by Vanessa Lemm.

Maurizio Ferraris, *Documentality: Why It Is Necessary to Leave Traces.* Translated by Richard Davies.

Dimitris Vardoulakis, *Sovereignty and Its Other: Toward the Dejustification of Violence.*

Anne Emmanuelle Berger, *The Queer Turn in Feminism: Identities, Sexualities, and the Theater of Gender.* Translated by Catherine Porter.

James D. Lilley, *Common Things: Romance and the Aesthetics of Belonging in Atlantic Modernity.*

Jean-Luc Nancy, *Identity: Fragments, Frankness.* Translated by François Raffoul.

Miguel Vatter, *Between Form and Event: Machiavelli's Theory of Political Freedom.*

Miguel Vatter, *The Republic of the Living: Biopolitics and the Critique of Civil Society.*

Maurizio Ferraris, *Where Are You? An Ontology of the Cell Phone.* Translated by Sarah De Sanctis.

Irving Goh, *The Reject: Community, Politics, and Religion after the Subject.*

Kevin Attell, *Giorgio Agamben: Beyond the Threshold of Deconstruction.*

J. Hillis Miller, *Communities in Fiction*.

Remo Bodei, *The Life of Things, the Love of Things*. Translated by Murtha Baca.

Gabriela Basterra, *The Subject of Freedom: Kant, Levinas*.

Roberto Esposito, *Categories of the Impolitical*. Translated by Connal Parsley.

Roberto Esposito, *Two: The Machine of Political Theology and the Place of Thought*. Translated by Zakiya Hanafi.

Akiba Lerner, *Redemptive Hope: From the Age of Enlightenment to the Age of Obama*.

Adriana Cavarero and Angelo Scola, *Thou Shalt Not Kill: A Political and Theological Dialogue*. Translated by Margaret Adams Groesbeck and Adam Sitze.

Massimo Cacciari, *Europe and Empire: On the Political Forms of Globalization*. Edited by Alessandro Carrera, Translated by Massimo Verdicchio.

Emanuele Coccia, *Sensible Life: A Micro-ontology of the Image*. Translated by Scott Stuart, Introduction by Kevin Attell.

Timothy C. Campbell, *The Techne of Giving: Cinema and the Generous Forms of Life*.

Étienne Balibar, *Citizen Subject: Foundations for Philosophical Anthropology*. Translated by Steven Miller, Foreword by Emily Apter.

Ashon T. Crawley, *Blackpentecostal Breath: The Aesthetics of Possibility*.

Terrion L. Williamson, *Scandalize My Name: Black Feminist Practice and the Making of Black Social Life*.

Jean-Luc Nancy, *The Disavowed Community*. Translated by Philip Armstrong.

Roberto Esposito, *The Origin of the Political: Hannah Arendt or Simone Weil?* Translated by Vincenzo Binetti and Gareth Williams.

Dimitris Vardoulakis, *Stasis before the State: Nine Theses on Agonistic Democracy.*

Nicholas Heron, *Liturgical Power: Between Economic and Political Theology.*

Emanuele Coccia, *Goods: Advertising, Urban Space, and the Moral Law of the Image.* Translated by Marissa Gemma.

Lightning Source UK Ltd.
Milton Keynes UK
UKHW010636280419
341725UK00005B/347/P